THE TAO OF

BRUCE LEE

Also by Davis Miller

The Tao of Muhammad Ali

THE TAO OF
BRUCE LEE

A Martial Arts Memoir

DAVIS MILLER

HARMONY BOOKS

NEW YORK

Published by Harmony Books, New York, New York. Member of the Crown Publishing Group.

Random House, Inc. New York, Toronto, London, Sydney, Auckland
www.randomhouse.com

HARMONY BOOKS is a registered trademark and the Harmony colophon is a trademark of Random House, Inc.

Chapters of this book have appeared in different forms in the *Independent on Sunday* (London), *Men's Journal, Arena* (England), *Esquire* (England), *M Quarterly* (Japan), and in *Panorama* (Australia).

Printed in the United States of America

Design by Leonard W. Henderson

Library of Congress Cataloging-in-Publication Data
Miller, Davis.
    The Tao of Bruce Lee : a martial arts memoir / by Davis Miller.
        p.   cm.
        1. Lee Bruce, 1940–1973.   2. Martial artists—United States—Biography.
3. Actors—United States—Biography.   4. Tao—Miscellanea.   5. Memoir.
I. Title.
GV1113.L44 M54 2000
791.43'028'092—dc21
[B]
                                                                            99-087697

ISBN 0-609-60477-5

10   9   8   7   6   5   4   3   2   1

First Edition

for Terry Davis

who has suffered through almost a quarter of a century
with this story and my writing.

Contents

Acknowledgments

Thanks first and foremost to Will Sulkin
without whom I'd still be a lowly sports writer

To Doug Pepper
The Man with the U.S. plan

To Jennifer Hunt
for holding me to the rigorous sweetness in this story

To Mel Berger
for not giving up this ghost

To George Tan
who has lived this story more than I

To Peter Nelson
for the right *Curse of the Dragon* contracts

And to
Aaron Copland, Dennis Kennedy,
Frank Lloyd Wright, Jidu Krishnamurti,
Siddhartha Gautama, Bodhidharma, Alan Watts,
Tom Simons

———

A ring center bow to Professor Joe Lewis

———

For my martial mentors: Tony Lopez, Kathy Long, Li Siu Loong,
Eric Nolan, John Chung

———

To Jesse Glover, and in memory of Ed Hart

———

To Dr. Donald Langford

———

To Muhammad Ali and "Sugar" Ray Leonard

———

To Laura Shepherd, Jan Wenner, Greg Williams, Bob Love, Kerry Shale,
Glenn Stout, John Rasmus, Tobias Perse

———

To Jerry Douglas, Béla Fleck, Edgar Meyer, and Russ Barenberg
for organic and uncategorizable musical inspiration.

———

To Harry Crews, Joan Didion, Nick Hornby, Tim O'Brien,
Tom Robbins, and Tom Wolfe for being pointing fingers.

———

To Holly Haverty-Woolson, for being my friend and for giving me one
of the best lines I've ever stolen.

———

*And to everyone who has let me know how much my Ali
stories have meant in their lives.*

Author's Note

I've been rigorous with what I've written of Bruce Lee's life. I have not, however, allowed day-to-day details to get in the way of the larger truth of *my own story*.

A story must take on its own reality, a kind of story-reality. No story is accurate; many tell the truth.

Parts of this tale don't fit with other stories. Look at the edges of even the "hardest," most immutable "facts." Look long enough, look honestly—the edges will shimmer.

Music's real. The rest is seeming.

—FATS WALLER

Dance as though no one is watching.

—PASSED ON BY DAVID HEBLER

Section One

ENTER THE FETUS

Show me a wonder
That you can't be sure of.

—FROM A SONG BY WALTER HYATT

One

O<small>N</small> M<small>ONDAY</small>, S<small>EPTEMBER</small> 27, 1973, I was a drowsy-eyed, twenty-one-year-old freshman at Lees-McRae Junior College in Banner Elk, North Carolina. It was a miserable time in my life. I had few friends, inside or outside class. I lived vicariously through *Superman* comic books and the outsized deeds of Muhammad Ali.

I was five-foot-seven and weighed ninety pounds. For a decade I had endured almost daily humiliation and bullying. Guys in my high school had nicknamed me "Fetus," a moniker which, after kids in the dorm read my senior annual, followed me to college. I was punched in the stomach, pushed into girls' restrooms, had my skinny bones stuffed into lockers, or was plain ignored. Although most of my contemporaries were preparing to graduate from university and proceed into the real world, I was maturing slowly (if, and there was real doubt about this, I was growing up at all).

That September marked the first time I'd been away from my father's house for longer than a weekend. I was homesick. To relieve my misery, I spent time in Banner Elk's only movie theater, drawn to the mystery and the power that lighted screens and hidden speakers have when placed at the front of large dark rooms.

Though Banner Elk's movie house was named the Center

Theater, Lees-McRae kids called it the Bijou. Had it not been for them, the village of fewer than three hundred residents could not have supported a cinema. Directly behind my dorm and at the end of the parking lot, the Bijou was about the size of, and maybe half as clean as, a greasy old two-car garage. Movies at the Bijou cost twenty-five cents. A different feature opened every three days. Since the beginning of the semester, I'd seen almost every movie that played at the Bijou.

The picture that night was *Enter the Dragon*. The house lights dimmed, flickered, went out. The red Warner Brothers logo flashed.

And there he stood.

There was a silence around him. The air crackled as the camera moved toward him and he grew in the center of the screen, luminous.

This man. My man. The Dragon.

One minute into the movie, Bruce Lee threw his first punch. With it, a power came roiling up from Lee's belly, affecting itself in blistering waves not only upon his on-screen opponent, but on the movie audience.

A wind blew through me. My hands shook; I quivered electrically from head to toe. And then Bruce Lee launched the first *real* kick I had ever seen. My jaw fell open like the business end of a dump truck. This man could fly. Not like Superman— better—his hands and his feet flew whistling through sky. Yes, better: this wasn't simply a movie, a shadowbox fantasy; there was a seed of reality in every Lee movement. Yet the experience of watching him felt just like a dream.

*   *   *

Bruce Lee was unlike anyone I (or any of us) had seen.

"It is not the vulgarity of James Arness pistol-whipping a drunken, stubbled stage robber," legendary folksinger Phil Ochs wrote of the first time he saw Bruce Lee. "It is not the ingenious devices of James Bond coming to the rescue, nor the ham-fisted John Wayne slugging it out in the saloon over crumbling tables and paper-thin imitation glass. It is the science of the body taken to its highest form, and the violence, no matter how outrageous, is always strangely purifying."

In *Enter the Dragon*, Bruce Lee moved fluidly, almost Alisweetblack, but with a rhythm distinctly his own. And, *oh!* was he fast. Even faster than Ali. So explosively quick that the paths of his hand-strikes were invisible. You could see techniques begin and end—nothing in the middle. It hardly seemed possible. Yet here he was, right in front of me, right here on this shimmering twenty-foot-tall screen.

Fists flying, feet soaring, punching and kicking bad guys from all angles. Punches and kicks—and much, much more. Lee's limbs moved in such a marvelously precise fashion that when he was facing the camera, his blows seemed to slice the screen into sections. In addition, he was the only genuinely lithe man I had ever seen, other than Ali. (Women were sometimes lithe, I believed; men almost never were.) Lee used hands and feet, knees and elbows, shoulders and head, *good great God, his entire body!* And he did so with just about perfect grace and balance.

Even more amazing: when he was standing still, something inside him vibrated; something continued to move.

Another big part of Lee's appeal for me was that he was only about my size. Though he seemed invulnerable, he was short and thin and there was a fragility, an eggshell mortality, about him. If this little bitty guy could be this righteous, whuppin' huge bad guys with such unthinkable speed, power, accuracy, and ratifying beauty, I could, too.

I was off to the moon.

Oh, hell, no! Not the moon. Neil Armstrong had already made that voyage. I was up, up, and away, on the first manned mission to Alpha Centauri.

* * *

Bruce Lee was a master of effortless effort, an artist whose brushstrokes sliced the air, and opponents' bodies, as naturally and unerringly as ancient Buddhist monks had spent only seconds stroking watercolors into bamboo patterns on rice paper, patterns that signified the Five Virtues of the Superior Man— simplicity, harmony, wisdom, contentment, a life beyond ambition.

Ali had seemed so singular, so freaky, such a mutant. And he was so damned huge. Bruce Lee's frame, the length of his arms and legs, the ratio of upper body to lower, looked almost exactly the same as my own, though I didn't consciously think about any of that.

What I knew in every molecule in my body was this: Bruce Lee was who I'd always wanted to be, what I'd always believed I could become (or, more precisely, *felt* I already was in some unseen way), although, before meeting Lee, I wasn't certain such a person could exist.

Two

THE END OF SUMMER of my eleventh year. As usual, I walk through the living room to the den. Though the sun hasn't cleared the tops of oaks and sycamores behind the house, aunts and uncles and grown-up cousins are sitting on our new green sofa and chairs, and are standing on the back porch smoking cigarettes.

My Aunt Anna and my father's Aunt Johnnie guide Carol and me to the kitchen table and bring us each a plate with a powdered white doughnut on it and a glass of watery orange juice that makes my stomach hurt. When we've eaten, Carol and I are led to our parents' room, where Daddy is seated on the bed. He pats the mattress on both sides of him, asking us to sit. Someone closes the door.

Daddy draws a deep breath. "God musta needed a blond-haired, blue-eyed angel," he says, calm and level.

Carol leans forward, looking at me from across Daddy's lap. "What does that mean?" she asks, her eyes sleepy, her mouth open, her voice soft and trusting.

"It means…" I hesitate; I'm not sure what it means. Then: "It means Mommy's dead," I say.

As the words leave my mouth, I know that they are true. A swarm of hornets rises in my chest and flies through me. My face stings, my hands do, too; so do my eyes. I run from the room, down the hall, into the kitchen. I stare out the alcove windows at cars passing on the street. How can everything look the same when all of it has changed forever?

"I'll kill them, I'll kill them all," I say, not knowing who I'm talking about, then knowing that, too. "I'll kill every doctor I ever see," I say.

And Aunt Anna comes and pulls me to her breasts and rocks me slow and gentle. "I'll kill every doctor in the world," I say through clenched teeth, not feeling my Aunt Anna at all.

And Daddy closes and locks the door to the room he'd shared with my mother. And he begins to wail and howl from somewhere so deep inside I could not have guessed such a place existed.

* * *

My mother, Sara Burns Miller, had died, age thirty-two, of a kidney disease we did not know she'd had, although she'd been sick all of my life. I've always believed that my mother's death is the most significant thing anyone could learn about me. And I also believe that it helps explain a great deal about how Muhammad Ali and then Bruce Lee came to be so important in my life.

My mother. Much of what I know about her can be found in the hundreds of photographs she took of me. These pictures share many qualities. I'm always dressed in doll-like perfect clothing. I'm almost always alone, standing glowing and perfectly formed in near-perfect light. I'm wearing a perfect camera-gobbling smile and have JFK-perfect hair: visible manifestations of my mother's compulsive ache for everything to be understood, in control, and, well, perfect (her health never was), an anxiety she passed on to me.

Within days of her death, I quit blaming doctors and placed the fault where it really belonged—on me. Mommy's doctor had advised her not to have children. But she had given birth to me and then to my sister. I thought Carol and I had made her die.

With this recognition, I shut myself away from everyone around me. When Daddy tried to talk with me, to pull me from my impermeable funk by asking questions, I answered not in words, but with grunts. By late November, when John Kennedy was killed, my catatonic force field was fully charged. By the spring of 1964 I'd not only quit talking, I'd just about stopped eating (during meals my stomach cramped so bad I'd fall to the floor, roll up in a ball, and rock back and forth in moaning pain), I'd quit playing with Carol and with other kids, and I came out of my shell only to watch Ali on Daddy's tiny black-and-white TV, to play by myself in the woods and down at the creek behind Daddy's house, to go to and from school (where I'd stopped doing work and sat staring at initials carved in my desktop, wondering when I'd wake from this awful dream), to buy comics and Tom Swift books, and to go to the movies.

The Carolina Theatre was the last of Winston-Salem's stately old movie palaces. Inside it was adorned with ornate silver sconces; marble statues of gods, goddesses and heroes; a wide, winding, red-carpeted staircase designed to make each of us, one and all, feel born of royalty; and a must-laden, stiff, faded, and stained once-red velvet curtain that looked as if it weighed a hundred tons.

On Saturday mornings at nine o'clock the dust-heavy curtain rose and, after paying ten cents admission, children twelve and under were shown a cartoon and a weekly episode of a Radar Man, Batman, or Superman serial; we played bingo for movie passes, popcorn, sodas, and candy; and we watched a full-length cowboy or monster picture.

On Friday and Saturday nights Daddy would take Carol and me to a western or a Disney. I remember a summer evening in 1964 when Carol was spending the night with a friend. I recall riding in the car with Daddy, and that the windows were down. Crickets and cicadas were throbbing; it was one of those nights so steamy and still that it seemed to float right up against your skin. I remember stopping for a cone of soft-serve vanilla ice cream on the way to a double feature at the Winston-Salem Drive-In. And, as the sticky ice cream dripped across my fingers, my father said, "Need to tell you 'bout these movies, son." His words, his tone, and the look on his face were obviously intended to carry weight.

"You'll see some things with women you never seen," he continued. I didn't understand what he meant, only that he sounded nervous, protective, and maybe a little guilty. "Nothin' to get worked up about, Dave," he assured me.

The movies that night were *Doctor No* and *Goldfinger*. Hours later, *entirely* worked up, I lay wide awake in bed, hearing the movie voices inside me, recalling not women on the screen, but how James Bond had been so screw-everybody cool, and how he'd disposed of all bad guys, effortlessly and systematically, the power magically vested in him by late-twentieth-century technology and by a strange, mystical Japanese science called karate.

A few weeks later, Daddy told me about a new TV show, *The Man from U.N.C.L.E.* We watched the first episode together. And here they were again, these secret-agent types, these coolest of the cool. To me, the hero, Napoleon Solo, was badder than Bond, cooler than zero, as he hiply and virtuously battled and almost effortlessly destroyed every foe, seldom, if ever, being hurt in return, having been rendered indestructible (and nonchalantly cocky!) by near-magical gadgetry, and by knowledge of that same exotic and miraculous "karate."

Over the next four years I ached to become Agent Solo. Weekday afternoons, until time for Daddy to get home from work, I crept from room to room in the house, shooting evil counter-agents (who fell bloodlessly dead before my eyes) and delivering lethal karate chops a hair's breadth away from lamps, bedposts, the hat rack beside the front door, and my favorite place of all—the back of the neck of the skinny, long-legged, trembling, female rat terrier my mother had bought and named Black Jet.

As five o'clock approached, I began to pace back and forth from my father's bedroom window to the kitchen alcove, watching for his car to come around the bend in the road. "Dear God," I'd plead to the walls and windows, "please let Daddy come home NOW."

In winter months it would be dark before I'd see the left-turn signal winking on his Impala. As the sun set, I'd get big anxious and large agitated. I'd race from bedroom to kitchen, kitchen to bedroom. As I ran from one end of the house to the other, when Carol got in the way, Jet wasn't the only one who suffered showers of karate chops.

On weekends I asked Daddy to drive me from pharmacy to toy store to department store, where I collected *Man from U.N.C.L.E.* accoutrements—trading cards, magazines, books, guns, badges, walkie-talkies, stereo LP records.

The Man from U.N.C.L.E. was last shown on NBC on January 15, 1968, my sixteenth birthday. To me, its passing was a major event. The year before, for refusing to be inducted into the army, Muhammad Ali had been stripped of his license to box; surely he was on his way to jail. I had no friends by then, only Napoleon Solo books, some pulpy boxing magazines, and the now darkened television.

*   *   *

All through my teen years, each weekday morning, after our father had fixed a hot breakfast for Carol and me and placed it on the table, he'd playfully march from the kitchen, down the hall, and into my room to wake me. All the way down the hall, he'd optimistically, rousingly, cheerfully sing. "Daaveee, Davy Crockett, King of the Wild Frontier," he'd serenade, cartoonishly exaggerating every syllable.

And "I can't get 'em up, I can't get 'em up, can't get 'em up in the morning. I can't get 'em up, I can't get 'em up, can't get 'em up at all." It may have been the only military song he knew. Daddy came of recruiting age after World War II. By the time American soldiers were fighting in Korea, he and my mother were married, I'd been born, and he was exempt from service. Thank goodness.

My father was such a wondrously gentle man, I believe that military training would've ruined him. Growing up stoically during the Depression and World War II in the industrial South—a place and time where there must have been considerable difficulty accepting his own sensitivity, much less regarding it as a virtue—the son of alcoholic parents, and losing his only childhood sweetheart when they were both so very young, I still marvel at his uncommon tenderness.

On weekday mornings, when Daddy tried to wake me, I couldn't open my eyes, couldn't force them open, not after ten, fifteen, twenty minutes, sometimes even half an hour. "Son, come on now," he'd say, trying to sound only a little irritated, "I'm gonna be late to work. Get on up and go splash some cold water on your face."

Many mornings, he'd take me by the hands, tug me from bed, lead me to the bathroom, turn on the water, splash it onto my face. No matter how hard I tried (and I did), I still couldn't open my eyes.

Three

MONDAY EVENING, SEPTEMBER 27, 1973, in the Banner Elk "Bijou." I watched—and heard and *felt*—Bruce Lee smack hundreds of people so hard and fast that they froze where they stood, their neurocircuitry scrambled. They bowed, they fell, they lay. And they didn't get up.

To me, this was high art and science; each moment, every movement, was rivetingly righteous, sanctifying, purifying—a steaming hot bath on a frozen night.

At the end of the last luxurious battle in *Enter the Dragon,* I looked at the world around me for the first time since Lee had appeared on screen. Compared to the song his body had sung, my existence was cold, mechanical, tedious. A moan, a Holden Caulfield whine.

I had no illusions about *Enter the Dragon* being a great film, or even a good one. It was more of the same Bondish junk I'd seen a thousand times and outgrown years before. *Enter* itself hadn't so affected me; it was Bruce Lee, who'd leapt, shining, from the screen.

As I left the theater, I didn't walk; I glided about a yard off the ground. As soon as I'd seen Lee, in that single incandescent moment, I knew: I had not even known what martial art was. Now an extraordinary new reality had been revealed. And that reality purred, for me, in a way nothing else had. What I had believed, abstractly, about who a martial artist could be had been defined, precisely, by Bruce Lee, this man who singlefistedly manifested so many of my ideals.

When I'd stumbled upon Lee in *Enter the Dragon,* I was a prospective monk finding an ancient Taoist scroll in the bargain bin at a small-town five-and-dime.

* * *

Enter left town on Thursday. But I needed more time with Lee. On Friday, instead of driving to my father's house, which I'd done every weekend since I'd started college, I tooled over to Johnson City, Tennessee, where the movie had been showing for a month and a half. At the door, a beautiful, dark-featured girl gave me a smile and a copy of a magazine called *Fighting Stars* that featured Lee on the cover. It was one of only a couple of times in my whole life that a good-looking girl had smiled at me.

What did it matter that she handed copies to people in front of me and behind? Those people were spectators, who floated from one sideshow to the next, seldom understanding—or curious to understand—whatever performance(s) they were seeing; wanting a performer, any performer, every performer (whether Lassie, Elvis, Sinatra, or Jesus), to deliver them, for a time, from boredom. I believed that I was different. This was the reason the beautiful girl had shared her smile with me.

Bruce Lee was a participant, a mover; I wanted to become one, too. And *Fighting Stars* would be the second chapter of my mystagogy; it would help introduce me to knowledge that might prove to be the peer of my well-worked martial pretensions.

Four

A<small>FTER WATCHING</small> *E<small>NTER THE</small> D<small>RAGON</small>* in Johnson City, I didn't know until I got back to my dorm room, opened the magazine cover, and read the hurriedly written obituary on page one—Bruce Lee was dead at age thirty-two.

I almost had to sit down on the floor. I couldn't see how or why someone so obviously alive could ever really die, at least at the age Lee had.

Thirty-two, the same age that Ali would be on his next birthday. And one year younger than Jesus had been when he'd been offed. Most important to me, though, it was the same age my mother had been when she'd died ten years before.

Christ, I wouldn't even've thought Lee was thirty-two. He looked mid-twenties, tops. A man so youthful, how could he be dead? Especially when he was the guy I'd hoped to find for so many years—and had only just met.

* * *

At sixteen, I was four-foot-ten, weighed sixty-three pounds, and felt powerless and forlorn almost all the time. It's an understatement to say that I had no interest in school. I flunked nearly every class on my schedule, I had failed the tenth grade (and would eventually fail the eleventh), and when Daddy tried to talk with me about doing something with my life, pleaded with me to get interested in anything, I told him that I already knew what I wanted and what I was qualified for—and I didn't need good grades to make it to the welfare rolls.

For my birthday present, hoping to capture The Power that Ali and Bond and Superman tapped into, I asked Daddy for karate lessons. The instructor we chose didn't look like Bond, Ali, or Superman; he was short, Italian, overweight, and by day worked as a hairdresser.

My father drove me to every karate class and I worked as hard as a sixty-three-pound runt could—punching and kicking the air in front of other skinny kids for an hour and a half, three nights a week; sweating and hurting under fluorescent lights that made my skin look splotched and blue.

Workouts stimulated my appetite and my confidence. I dressed spiffy and made friends. "Kid Karate," girls wrote in my junior yearbook. The year before, no one had signed my annual; the few guys who'd talked to me had called me "Piss-ant" and "Fetus."

During karate class, the big, round hairdresser/instructor told us of great spiritual powers he possessed, and about little Japanese gents who catch arrows in midflight, break concrete blocks with their heads, punch through watermelons, chew and swallow glass, kill with single, seemingly ordinary touches. Whenever Sensei was asked to demonstrate his skills, he gracefully declined, explaining that The Secrets were too powerful to show to just anyone.

So. I kept sweating and hurting and kicking and punching

and sweating under the lights, hoping to become good enough to learn The Secrets.

And Sensei kept telling his stories. The one about the old, shriveled and blind Buddhist monk who lived near Kyoto, and who had fought in, and been the survivor of, over fifteen hundred one-on-one death matches. And the one about Count Nakamura, who'd been blessed with the gift of The Iron Palm by one of the ancients; no one could survive one of Count Nakamura's Iron Palm strikes. And of the many immortal, invincible Japanese masters, whose eyes radiated a strange white heat and upon whom no one dared look.

I believed the stories. I needed to.

After a year and a half of blistering work, practicing stances and forms, flicking hand-strikes and kicks at mirrors in class and for an hour alone in my bedroom every night, I earned a brown belt, the rank immediately below black. In the interim, I'd grown to be a five-foot-tall, eighty-pound stud, after finally reaching puberty. I'd soon learn one of The Secrets.

Not from my hairdresser/karate sensei, but from Alvin Lindsor.

Alvin was the second-smallest kid at school. He weighed eighty-eight and was two years younger than I, though we were in the same grade. He was a standout member of the varsity wrestling squad, fought with the Gladiators amateur boxing team, stole beer from 7-Elevens, and whupped up on bigger kids in his spare time. No one dared call Alvin by anything but his name.

The high school Alvin and I attended, Mount Tabor, was housed in a brand-new, one-story brick building, the institutional equivalent of 1960s ranch-style houses. Mount Tabor was the Winston-Salem/Forsyth County School Board's experiment in progressive education. Basic English, math, and health classes were taught by television sets. Sports history was offered as an alternative to senior English. Troublemakers weren't kept after school in teachers' offices or classrooms. Minor offenders—those rampant hormone cases who'd been caught chucking spit wads at Mr. Evans, the gay biology teacher, chomping gum in Mr. Morris's English lit. class, arriving tardy for Miss Ooten's homeroom, or hunkering over fifteen-year-old Julia "Jugs" Jordan's rather obvious physical virtue(s)—would report to Detention Study Hall promptly at three-fifteen, where they'd spend the next sixty minutes. Detention Study Hall was housed in the cafeteria. Alvin and I were charter members.

DSH, as we habituals called it, was founded on the hopeful assumption that if strays were herded into a central holding pen where they'd be overseen by a single trail boss, cowhands would be free to complete their chores unhampered. I first suspected The Secret in DSH. It was a Monday afternoon in February 1971 and I was serving a sentence for refusing to dress-out in phys. ed. (I didn't dare undress in front of anybody, anywhere, even if a teacher said that I had to and even if all the people around me were just guys.)

I was sleeping at the far end of a yellow Formica-topped table, and when I woke and looked up, Alvin, who'd been sitting near the opposite end when I'd gone to sleep, was standing over me, holding my history book open in front of my face. Spit was rolling from its pages.

He closed the book, laid it on the table, walked to his seat, slapped hands with a couple wrestler buddies, and sat down beside Sam Stone. Stone was short and bunchy-muscled and had the same burning steel-gray eyes that I envisioned the great karate masters having. And Stone was twenty-one years old and was in the eleventh grade. My sophomore year, when sitting beside him in DSH, he'd ripped a sleeve from my red alpaca sweater and cut a quarter-inch-deep hole in my back with his pocket knife, all for fun. It was stuff like that, and the magma in his eyes, that made everybody think that Stone was a genuine maniac.

Out of the corner of my eye I saw Stone pass Alvin something, maybe a note, under the table. Alvin glanced down at it, then rose from his seat and ambled over. I began to sweat. Stone was looking past Alvin and at me. There was a glint in his eyes.

Alvin glared down hard at me, then lowered his right hand to my bony excuse for a left biceps, which he squeezed a little, before sliding it across the shoulder of my crisply starched, almost brand-new "Beau Brummel" shirt (the more starch, the stiffer the exoskeleton, the more substantial the man), and up to the collar, which he wrenched into a knot. I reached to straighten it. Alvin slapped down my hand.

"Hey, you, you fuckin' Fetus, you. You got a lotta people fooled, actin' like you got some karate corncob stuck up your ass. But me and Stone, we know what a pussy you are." He thrust a jaggedly bitten fingernail a couple inches from my nose. "Tomorrow I'm gonna make you eat shit off that corncob, turdface."

Mr. Hayes, the gym teacher who'd made me stay after school, was in charge of DSH that week. He didn't look up from the magazine he was reading. Alvin's friends laughed. Long, high, cackling laughter that made my arms and legs feel frozen stiff to the ground.

*   *   *

I skipped first period the next morning. When I walked into homeroom, everyone was talking about the inevitable "War of the Midgets." At Mount Tabor, Miller-Lindsor would be as much the Fight of the Century as the Muhammad Ali–Joe Frazier bout that would take place in less than two weeks.

Most students and a few teachers were placing bets on who'd win. Rumor had it that Mr. Cole, the wrestling coach, had twenty dollars on Alvin. Supposedly so did the principal, Mr. Hearty, who'd been a Golden Gloves boxer. Fourteen-year-old Batman, Green Hornet, and James Bond fans were betting their quarters on me.

To get out of second-period study hall, I volunteered to deliver mimeographed copies of the list of absentees to teachers. Alvin and my sister were in the same Spanish class. Carol was sitting close to the front of the room. Along with the other hard-asses, Alvin was near the back, using his hands to play the drum solo from "Wipe Out" on his desktop.

Miss Rapley, the Spanish teacher, was the only black woman who taught at Mount Tabor. And she was my favorite person in the whole school. I had Spanish with Miss Rapley fourth period, before lunch. Every Friday she played Santana records in class and told us stories about her college internship in Argentina. She'd wander from desk to desk, singing songs in that beautiful language that made her better than us. One Monday a couple weeks before the end of the year, Miss Rapley suddenly wasn't in class and Mr. Hearty was telling us that she wouldn't be back. She'd been busted for her nighttime and weekend business—selling marijuana out of her little garage apartment across from campus. After Mr. Hearty introduced us to our new teacher, I walked out of class and never came back. For the rest of the year I took a double lunch period so I could nap longer and then maybe wander the halls.

This February morning, though, when I passed Alvin on the way up to Miss Rapley's desk, some guy I didn't know, sitting next to Carol, yelled, "There's that Karate Kid Miller that Alvin's gonna beat crap out of."

"Alvin couldn't whup me with a baseball bat," I said almost instantly, not only to impress Miss Rapley and to defend my pride and my family's, but in defense of the Japanese martial arts.

Guys laughed and made *ooh*ing sounds and somebody behind Alvin pushed his shoulders, prodding him on. Miss Rapley slipped an arm around my shoulders and escorted me from the room, gently closing the door behind me.

*   *   *

"Here, catch," shouts the man. He's standing several yards away. I'm not wearing my glasses; I can't see his face. A long wooden object tumbles toward me, a couple feet over my head. I try to grab it. My timing isn't good. The wind sings through it as it passes by my hands; it makes a plopping sound as it drops into the perfect middle of a pool of water behind me. I don't realize until I turn and see Silas Creek that I'm standing

near the end of my father's backyard. The object floats down-
stream. I reach into my trousers pockets, find my glasses, put
them on.

The man has disappeared. The object is a bamboo flute. I
want that instrument. I feel the need to learn to play.

I stand on the bank, scared to jump into the stream. Even
though I know the water will feel ssooo *fine. I'm scared of*
what may lie beneath the surface—jagged thrusting rocks,
giant jutting shards of glass, knife-finned carp, alligator snap-
ping turtles, sea snakes, dragons, Ninjas, mud, Joe Frazier, my
mother.

And I'm scared because I don't know how to swim. But the
water in the creek is never deeper than waist level, even after
the worst summer storms. I follow the flute as it floats down-
stream, tumbling over and around rounded stones, making
musical bumping sounds. The current isn't fast; there's no need
to run. It's easy to walk along the bank and stay parallel to the
rolling bamboo flute.

But why do I find it so hard to jump in? Particularly if I
want the instrument so bad.

*   *   *

I didn't go to school the next two days. Usually, when I skipped
class, I stayed in the building, creeping down the halls from one
bathroom to the next, combing my hair and throwing hand-
strikes at my reflection in the mirrors above the sinks.

This time was different. I could say I had a purpose. I pretended to be sick until Daddy left the house, then I got out of bed
and worked out hard both days—and both nights in Sensei's

class—making myself look forward to the grand opportunity that Alvin had given me to showcase my rarefied skills.

Tiger Claws, Dragon Rakes, Dream Fists. Prisms of light leap effortlessly from my fingertips. Alvin falls before me and is grateful to have received a lesson in the fistic mysteries from his obvious superior.

Friday morning, I dressed in the pants to my green pinstripe suit and took extra time combing my hair so I'd look pretty for the fight. Daddy drove Carol and me to school. He let us out at the entrance, and Carol went ahead of me. As I opened the door to the building, an "honor guard" of wrestlers and football players appeared from wherever they'd been waiting. They escorted me to Alvin, standing with a large pack of friends around the corner.

I cocked my head to the side and put on my very best swagger for him. He sneered at me. "Good mornin', faggot," he spat. "How come you never go out with no wimmin? You like men better, don't you, faggot?"

Before I had a chance to say anything, he slapped me, hard, on the right cheek. My glasses flew from my face and ricocheted with a hollow metal sound off the row of lockers behind me.

I felt The Secret then, first in my stomach, next in my throat, but I pretended it wasn't there and shoved it back in my belly. "Hey, man, not in here," came a voice from somewhere. "Take him to the parking lot."

Someone passed me my glasses. I put them on; they were lopsided. I remember floating out the door and across the asphalt, feeling the crowd grow around us. Alvin led me to the end of the lot and up a short grassy hill, where we stopped in front of a stand of yellowed scrub pines. I glanced behind me at the sea of people. All two thousand Mount Tabor students, *and their parents!*, had to be. I handed my glasses to a stranger. Jesus, what a bunch of faces. "Break his ribs, Alvin." Faces, full with a mean kind of joy.

I lowered myself into the deep, strong, bent-legged horse-stance I'd practiced for what seemed endless hours in karate class (legs so far spread it looked as if I were trying to straddle the Pacific Ocean), and chambered both fists in the inverted *hachiji-dachi* position on the waist, elbows flat against the sides, chest thrust out, neck high and rigid, exactly the way Sensei had taught.

Alvin stared at me incredulously, until he realized that I intended to fight from that stance. Then his eyes relaxed. "You gonna try'n kick me, pussy?" he said, smiling, and he tucked his chin in next to his shoulder and raised both fists to ear level. "Only girls and faggots kick each other," he said, laughing.

He took two steps to the left and I turned with him, determined to face him no matter where he moved. He pushed his open left palm into my nose, pulled it back. I kept both fists at my sides. He slapped me across the mouth, and again. I tried to deflect the second blow with the rising, looping, outside *age-uke* block I'd been taught in class. It was too stiff and too slow. Alvin jabbed me, close-fisted, and hooked off it. The punches didn't hurt, only numbed my face. I kept both fists chambered at the waist. Alvin slid two more jabs into my chin; my head twice slammed the back of my shoulders. He laughed once more. Much of the crowd laughed with him. Their laughter thundered over me. Soon I was lost in the thunder.

Alvin tackled me at the waist; I fell jarringly onto my shoulders, then rolled down the hill. He followed, jumping onto my chest, pinning my arms, and punching both sides of my face. I felt the first shot bounce my head off the grass to the left, the second one to the right, before I managed to yank my arms free and grab his wrists, which I held, white-knuckled, until somebody screamed, "Teacher."

Alvin sprang from my chest and shape-shifted into the crowd. The guy who was holding my glasses put them on my face, pulled me to my feet, told me to run. I stumbled into the pines, still reeling in the thunder, until Mr. Evans retrieved me and led me to the principal's office. Swimmy-headed, I told Mr. Hearty that I thought Sam Stone had offered Alvin money to start the fight. He summoned Stone, told me to go to class. I left the building and walked home.

When Daddy came in from work, he took one look at me and said, "Don't take an ass-kickin' again, son. Even if you have to pick up a stick and crack 'em in the head with it."

I promised that I wouldn't.

That night, lying in bed, staring up into the dark with my face throbbing, I realized that in the two years I had attended karate class, not once had anyone fought. Not once had anyone made contact with anything solid. Not once had I punched or kicked anything other than a whole lot of air and dreams.

Monday at school, Batman fans and my new friends asked

why I hadn't kicked Alvin or punched him back. I shrugged. How could I tell them I didn't know how?

I never returned to fat hairdresser/Sensei's karate class. And it wasn't long after my fight with Alvin that kids at school started calling me Fetus again.

Five

Entries in my 1971 Mount Tabor High School annual:

Karate Man, ALIAS Pussyman, ALIAS PIS-ANT,
The karate expert of MTH. Telling all the lies and me beleiving them. You've made up some good ones. You are one lieing little sack of shit. I'm glad Lindsor gave you what was coming to you, you stupid jerkoff.

Rodgers

Fetus,
Who the fuck you think you are? You grew another 1/100 of a inch this year and 1/16 of a pound. How's karate? Me and you will have to have a fight sometime. It's been fun beating Hell out of you in homeroom. Even when you finally manage to graduate, your gonna be nothin but a little turd. Kiss one big rosey red ass, you future street bum.

Gentle

Six

"**B**RUCE LEE MAY BE THE WORLD'S BEST-conditioned athlete," a *Fighting Stars* story announced to movie patrons of North America, "and its most dynamic living martial artist."

I know that, I thought, reading the story in my dorm room. Lee told me so himself, through the luster of his actions. Tell me something I don't know, like how I can get there, too.

"There are Malaysian tribes who worship him as a god," Alex Ben Block claimed in a story he wrote for the August 1973 issue of *Esquire,* for sale in stores on the twentieth of July, the date that Lee had died. I'd bought a copy of *Esquire* that month when I was bored hanging out with Daddy as he shopped for groceries, but didn't pay much attention to the Lee article until I remembered it after seeing *Enter.*

As soon as I was through with *Fighting Stars,* I pulled the *Esquire* from my sock drawer and read it thoroughly. I learned all sorts of fan-boy stuff. Bruce Lee had been born in 1940, a Chinese year of the dragon (I, too, had been born in a year of the dragon, 1952); hence his nickname in Hong Kong, *Li Siu Loong,* "Small Dragon Lee." I'd later learn that the dragon is the most powerful—and most benevolent—creature in Chinese mythology.

Enter the Dragon was the vehicle designed to introduce Lee to American audiences. He was married; his wife, Linda, was Caucasian-American; they had two children. Lee was Chinese-American (he was one-fourth European, as are Ali and I); he'd studied philosophy at the University of Washington; had played Kato in the *Green Hornet* TV series (I'd missed him—and maybe enlightenment—because the show was aired opposite *The Man from U.N.C.L.E.* in 1966); and Lee was "too unorthodox to suit most of the conservative karate establishment."

Block's piece alluded to three movies that Lee had made for Hong Kong audiences; but the story had little of the fresh-squeezed martial juice I was hoping for, though its tone suggested such nourishment did exist. It had been designed to tease more than to enlighten, as had *Enter the Dragon* itself. Which would've been great, if Lee hadn't died. But as things were, I found more sustenance in the accompanying photographs. (With Lee, one most always finds more in image than anywhere else.)

I cut out the best pictures from both magazines and pasted them to pieces of black construction paper, which I taped to the wall beside the Ali poster opposite my bed, where I'd see them each night before I went to bed, and each morning when I woke.

Seven

THE (FIRST) RESURRECTION of Muhammad Ali occurred in late 1970. At first, since I no longer watched TV, Ali existed only as a name I overheard in scraps of conversation: "...that bull-shittin', uppity nigger Clay," light-haired, fair-skinned country boys spat as I passed them in the Mount Tabor halls between classes.

But he seeped back in. Yes. Slowly. Because I felt the bruises that Alvin had given me. And I wasn't certain I wanted to, or even could, believe in heroes anymore.

I remember a morning near the end of February 1971, about a week after I'd been trounced by Alvin and a few days before the first Ali-Frazier bout. Daddy was driving Carol and me to school, and the 7:20 sports report was on the radio. Ali was being interviewed after a training session. "The real king is back," he roared. "Joe Frazuh ain't nothin' but a pretender to my throne."

My father looked at me, chuckling. "There's your man," he said, reaching to turn up the volume (though he would've had no interest in Ali if it weren't for me). And when he did, Ali's voice rose and rang and punched a hole through the chrome-covered speaker. One thing I'd not forgotten was Ali's voice.

The whole time he'd been kept from boxing, I'd practiced his smoky Southern song in front of mirrors at home and in big-echoing bathrooms at school.

"Joe Frazuh ain't no contest for a scientific boxer like me. Gowna beat that man *sooo baaddd* about his head and shoulders. Now this might shock and amaze ya, but I'm gowna destroy Joe Frazuh."

On fight night, although Ali-Frazier was shown live only at closed-circuit locations, on their news programs all three national TV networks broadcast classic moments from Ali's mid-sixties bouts. Without clips from his fights, I couldn't have comprehended what I'd forgotten. Ali had seemed a fantasy from another time, an impossible and chimerically cheesy myth, like Agent Solo, like Superman's invulnerability, or like growing up with a healthy, happy, and nurturing mom.

How could anyone let six popping punches fly in a single second? Sensei had instructed us always to throw only one blow and to deliver it only from the rear arm. Only the rear arm had any true power in it. Yet right in front of my eyes Ali was doing it, punching real, live human beings with near-invisible speed with both hands. And he punched effortlessly and seemed *never* to miss, gliding about the ring as gracefully as the pantherlike karate masters fat Sensei had imagined. Here he was on my TV screen, Muhammad Ali, the Black Superman, so much more than my shadowy memories of him.

That night I went to bed with my transistor radio tucked under my pillow. When I'd switched off the lights, I pulled it out, tugged the stiff leather strap up around my wrist, placed the leather-covered speaker against my ear, and spun the tiny plastic dial back and forth until I found an announcer who was summarizing each round of the fight after it had been fought. A little after midnight he said that Frazier had won a decision. Although I didn't believe him, I wept.

Within days, though, Ali made me feel better when he told the world he hadn't really lost. "Hit Joe Frazuh six times for every time he hit me. Joe Frazuh stayed in the hospital two weeks after the fight. *Maannn,* I sent Joe Frazuh to the hospital for two solid weeks."

So. I found myself standing in front of mirrors around the house again, flipping my wormy left arm toward the reflection, trying to replicate Ali's hot and sweet snake-lick jab. My romance with martial art returned, and I began to work on variations of some basic karate hand-strikes, applying what I could understand of Ali's boxing style to help loosen up the stiff Japanese techniques. I practiced *sansen-tsuki,* which translates as "fighting blow," the first punch karate beginners are taught. *Sansen-tsuki* is thrown from the full-frontal *hachiji-dachi* position, fists inverted and on the waist, knees bent and legs spread as if you were trying to strapple railroad tracks.

Instead of keeping my fists closed tight, as Sensei had taught, I held my hands loose and open ever so slightly, like Ali's. I turned to the left to present a smaller target, tucked my chin in low next to my shoulder, raised my right hand to ear level, dangled the left one at my side (jabs can be popped loose and snappy and much faster from waist height), stationed my legs a couple feet apart, and bent them just a little at the knees. Behind my heat-seeking jab, I worked on slinging as many twisting *sansen-tsuki* as I could in two seconds, concentrating on throwing punches not in rote patterns like Sensei, but in unpredictable rhythms and groupings.

Throughout the spring of 1971, I practiced my punches about three days out of every seven, but then, since I longed to be accepted by other Mount Tabor guys (most of whom thought that the coolest of the cool, the real men, were ones who stayed drunk half the time), I caught a case of teenage dipsomania.

That summer I drank and drank, until I built up enough tolerance to down a daily six-pack of Miller Malt Liquor, wanting people to associate the famous name with my own. All the eighty-pound, nineteen-year-old drunks I've known are fairly incapable of organized, rapid, sustained, physical activity. Instead of training to become more like Ali, I settled for a tentative flick or two from my left fist every time I passed a mirror.

I began smoking cigars, fat ol' stogies nearly twice as big around as my thumb. I didn't inhale the smoke, just sucked it in and blew it out, the cigar hanging out of the corner of my mouth, my left arm hooked around a rolled-down car window, trying to look cool perched up high on the seat cushion I needed to see over the steering wheel, even as discharged smoke found its stinging way into my eyes. I bought cigars in ten-cent packs of six that barely fit into the starched pockets of my boys' size-12 shirts. And I completed my look by wearing English-style Ben Hogan golf caps at the accepted cool Southern angle, brim high and slightly to the left of my nose, cap tilted fifteen degrees left of level.

I tried to join the Polish Drinking Team, a fraternal and elitist group of ballplayers and wrestlers that had been founded and was led by Frank Romanosky and Ken Wesolowsky, both of whom had been born to Russian parents. Romo and Weso were renowned for borrowing Weso's old man's bulldog's collar and leash and leading each other around on all fours, barking and growling at women in the halls, at bars, and in fast-food places.

> *Fetus, glad you didn't make it to the PDT,*
> *you godamed pussy. It sure would be nice to*
> *anitiate your scrawny little ass anyway.*
> *Arfmann(ski)*

*   *   *

All through my high school years, I took two to three showers every day; each time I passed a sink I scrubbed my hands, which became pink, then chapped, then scaly. I washed my hair nightly and, when I stepped from the shower, left it dripping wet, soaking it further with one-fifth of a can of hair spray, combing out the curls I'd inherited from my mother, then letting it dry helmet-hard and sleeping on it. First thing in the mornings, I spent a quarter of an hour brushing out the crusty spray. And hoped that my hair was straight and I looked normal like other guys at school.

I bought clothes with every cent of my allowance I hadn't committed to beer and cigars. I owned probably two dozen sweaters (boys' size 14) and pairs of trousers (14 slim), and twice that many shirts. The clothes hangers in my closet were equidistantly spaced. Long-sleeved shirts were organized by colors and were separated from short sleeves and from trousers. Ten or so golf caps were stored side by side on the high shelf of the closet; each day of the week I'd hide my hair under a different color cap. My closet floor was lined with pair after pair of (size 4½) dress shoes. Every night, when I took off the shoes I'd worn that day, I polished them until they gleamed more brightly than brand-new. Trousers were professionally dry-cleaned and pressed, I never wore jeans or T-shirts, and I'd not put on a shirt that didn't have about ten pounds of starch in it. I felt a need to remain not only crisp but spotless. Unsoiled. Clean, every moment.

In early July, before my senior year, Daddy bought a three-year-old, 327/four-barrel turquoise Camaro that sported its original tires and only twelve thousand miles on the odometer. "Would want one of these if I was your age, son," he said, passing me the keys. On his small salary as a foreman in a plant that made corrugated boxes in which cartons of R.J. Reynolds cigarettes were packed, my father couldn't afford such an expensive car. I knew that he'd bought it to make me feel better, to help me find a life. And I was grateful—or as grateful as anyone can be when he's dead asleep. I promised Daddy that I'd take special care of the car.

The rest of that summer and through the fall, I washed the Camaro twice a week, every week, spent an hour or so cleaning the interior each time it was washed, and I waxed it every second week. Its black vinyl interior always shone. The turquoise paint beaded water better than anybody else's car I knew. At night, even when it wasn't raining, the Camaro looked wet with city lights and polyurethane. Everybody wanted to ride in my Camaro. Even ones who didn't like me. And I didn't mind giving people rides. But I didn't let anybody use the ashtrays, and everyone had to wipe their feet before placing them on the floor mats. At least I pretended I could make them do those things.

That summer I had my biggest growth spurt ever. I got all the way to five-foot-three, and even broke eighty pounds. But in the fall few people noticed. I still needed my seat cushion to see over the steering wheel.

*   *   *

On the second Friday of October, Weso and Romo asked me for a ride to the football game so they could get good and juiced without worrying which of them would drive. I thought football was the dumbest sport going, all those fat-asses standing out in the light for everybody to see, wearing all those fat-ass pads and stupid uniforms and helmets and a ball and rules and shit. But everybody at Mount Tabor went to the games. And, man, did I want to be like everybody else.

The night before the game, we made a couple gallons of Purple Jesus and stored it in the trunk of the Camaro. Staring out the window in geometry class, I could see it patiently waiting for us, ripening and getting devoutly toxic.

I washed and waxed the Camaro after school, and spent two whole dollars filling up with gas. It was gray and cold that Friday, and clouds were round and silver and rolling like ones you'd expect to see in *Jason and the Argonauts* or *The Ten Commandments*. Just the right clouds and weather for football, even if I did hate the stupid goddamn sport.

When I was ready to leave the house around six-thirty, every detail looked right for a fine Friday night. I slipped my fingers around the steering wheel, patted the gas pedal, turned the key in the ignition, and felt the engine hum all the way from my fingers to my toes. I slid my Stylistics tape into the 8-track player, popped the transmission into first and purred on down the road, getting off on my sweet soft soul sounds and admiring the streetlight reflections on my fresh-waxed hood.

I picked up the two self-proclaimed Polacks, then tooled on over in the direction of the stadium. They were both dipping deep into the vat of PJ and were pretty wasted before we got to the game. We parked the car and moved off behind the stadium, away from the lights and into a stand of scraggly pines and dogwoods. The patch of woods was cold. The smell of wet fallen leaves enveloped us. We quickly found a place where we couldn't see the parking lot; bunches of ground-out cigarette butts were at the base of the fence. When I'd climbed halfway, I noticed that Romo wasn't with us. I turned and looked for him and couldn't see through the trees. I jumped from the fence and stepped out from the woods into salmon-pink light from the big fluorescents.

There he was, about fifty yards from the Camaro, in the middle of a shining circle of shattered glass where nobody'd parked. Around him stood a gaggle of ten or so chest-high, maybe thirteen-year-old black kids. And Romanosky was in a sort of pseudo-*kiba-dachi* stance, right fist fully extended at shoulder height, the other inverted on the hip. And he was making some kind of dumb squealing noise and was hopping up and down like a radioactive rooster.

I sprinted across the parking lot to help. After all, if anybody understood blacks, it was me. I dressed black, walked black, talked black. Ali was my man, Miss Rapley was the coolest person I'd ever met, and I was the Mount Tabor High king of soul music.

As I ran toward Romo, I heard Weso's big feet clunking up behind. I made it there first, even with my short-ass legs.

"Hey, cuz, what's goin' on?" I asked the tallest and blackest of the kids, the one as big as me who seemed to be the leader.

He ignored me. "Here comes your white-ass cavalry, Mister Karate Man," he said to Romo, sporting the coldest grin I had ever seen. We were only a few miles south of the downtown R.J. Reynolds plants. The sweet, overripe smell of piss-gold broadleaf was on the air. It was a smell that had always made me feel sick to my stomach. I pulled at Frank's sleeve. His longish cheeks looked tight and sunken. One of them trembled every few seconds. It was cold; you could see his breath in the air. His reddish hair was stuck by sweat to his temples; his skin looked clammy.

"Come on, Romo, let's go," I said. "Come on, now, don't nobody want no trouble." I felt glass crunch under my shoes.

And the big black kid hit me on the stomach with a bag of nickels he'd been hiding somewhere. I heard it jangle and figured what it was. But it didn't hurt. I guess he didn't know how to angle a punch.

Why'd you do that? I wanted to ask. Look at my clothes. Hear my voice. Go to my ride, check out the sounds I listen to. Can't you tell how hip I am? Don't look at my face. That ain't me. Can't you tell I'm a lot like you? Can't you see these clowns use me, too?

And the black kid tried to hit me again. That's when I had the Ali flashback. The kid's chin appeared like a lighted window in a darkened wall. Everything else disappeared.

Before he got his bag-slow fist halfway around, I stabbed him, flat on the bridge of the nose, with two hard left jabs. Just like the ones Ali'd impaled Cleveland Williams on. Where had those come from? I'd only imagined *Ali* throwing the punches. If I'd thought about *me* doing it, I would've gotten scared and wouldn't've been able to.

The blows had come out so smooth and easy, just like The Champ's. And then the boy was lying down. And there was blood everywhere; everywhere there was blood. From out of his nostrils, around his mouth, down his chin and holey white T-shirt, it flowed. There was a small puddle of it on the asphalt and glass beside his head.

I looked for Weso: he was running for the car. Romo stood kind of beside me, off to the left, in that stupid *kiba-dachi* someone had shown him. "Go ahead," another black kid was saying, "try some of your ka-raw-ti shit." No one knew that I'd hit their friend.

I grabbed Romo by the arm and pulled him hard, spinning him toward me. "The car," I said, "go to the car," and I dug my feet in and took off running. Frank beat me to the Camaro and I threw him the keys. He unlocked the door on the passenger's side and he and Weso slid together onto the bucket seat. One of them opened my door for me.

I jumped in behind the wheel. We locked both doors and tried to rip out of there. A big black Buick pulled in the way and blocked the exit. Another dark car fell in behind.

I couldn't back up, couldn't go forward. There I sat with my foot on the brake while the hive of dirty, sweaty thirteen-year-olds descended on my cleanmeancoolblue ride. They swarmed all around, whirling up and down on the fenders, smearing street-soiled fingers all over my fresh-Windexed windows. And then the kid I'd hit was there, blood pouring from his nose, green shining shards of glass sticking out of his cheek, standing beside my door with steam rolling out his mouth. And he had an almost empty Rebel Yell bottle coiled in his fist, the bottle not yet a part of the hand, his hand still young and moldable-looking, looking like it should be holding a couple slices of Sunbeam bread with peanut butter chunked up in between.

He swung and broke the bottle on the window next to my face. I jumped and got both hands up beside my head, but the window didn't shatter. Weso or Romo or both of them yelled, "There's some cops, over there."

I looked where they pointed. Not a hundred yards away, there they stood, two of them, both white, directing traffic with big orange flashlights, looking as bored as the kids in remedial English class. I blew the horn once, twice, held it down. The big black kid was kicking the hell out of my door. Two other kids were pounding on the hood. One cop looked up, said something at his partner, pulled out his stick, and jogged methodically toward us. I saw a lot of legs dart past, turned and watched thirteen-year-olds fly off in some ten different trajectories.

The Buick in front of us finally moved. I pulled onto the street, over to the curb, climbed out, and told my story to the second cop. He looked sleepy and kept directing traffic.

"Well, what do you expect me to do, son?" he said in his best dismissive cop voice. "Something like this happens most every weekend."

Yeah, I thought, but you're missing the point. The point is it doesn't happen to me and my Camaro—and you're not a very nice guy to be a peace officer. "Look at these giant dents all over my car," is all I said.

"Go on about your business, son," he answered.

*   *   *

To calm down, we drove around awhile, each taking a couple dips into the vat of PJ. When we figured the game was over, we headed for Staley's, a burger joint that had been the postgame hangout for at least a thousand years.

About halfway there, Weso clapped me on the shoulder. "Goddamn, Davis, didn't know you had it in you," he said. "You know, you've gotten real good at that judo stuff."

I smiled and pushed my golf cap farther back from my brow. He'd called me "Davis." I couldn't remember the last time anybody'd called me by my name, except my father and sister. To everybody else I was Fetus, or Runt, or Mouse, or Shrimp, or Tadpole, or Pissant, or something besides me.

"What belt you got now, anyway, a black?"

I didn't say that what I'd done wasn't any kind of Asian martial art. Or that it had happened mostly by accident. And that if it had anything to do with anybody, my mentor was Ali. I just kept on smiling and driving.

*   *   *

In celebration of my act of good-ol'-boy heroism, I was admitted to the Polish Drinking Team. Romo and Weso presented me with a jersey at a special meeting at the hospitality room of the

Schlitz brewery out off Highway 109. The shirt was royal blue; my name and title had been stenciled on in big yellow block letters above my official number, "00." Royal blue and yellow: the Mount Tabor colors. The shirt read PISSANT-SKI, DRILL INSTRUCTOR. I tried it on. It was only a million sizes too big.

Every Friday, I proudly wore the jersey as if it were a letter sweater—I had my starched shirt on underneath. PDT meetings took place on Friday nights at Sam's Tavern on the Green. Soon it was February and time to order caps and gowns. A form was given to seniors requesting correct spelling of names for graduation programs. I printed mine as "Davis Worth Miller," then added "the third," which, of course, was a lie. But I thought that it made me sound cool, made me special.

In the area provided for honors and activities, I listed myself as Drill Instructor for the Polish Jerkoff Team, Alvin Lindsor's sparring partner, and charter member of Detention Study Hall. When Daddy asked to attend my graduation, I told him I'd decided not to go. But I didn't tell a single person at school.

*   *   *

That fall, everybody enrolled in college, or got a job, or joined the military and ended up in Vietnam. I didn't do any of those things. Every day, first thing when I woke, I'd pull the Camaro out of the driveway and head for Highway 158. If it was lunchtime, I'd hear the twelve-thirty freight moaning up ahead and I'd go left, following the sound and the tracks up The Strip, past tobacco and cotton and cornfields, vegetable stands and feed stores, thundering around old slow-going Ford and Chevy pickups, up where 158 became Stratford Road and kudzu vines stopped creeping so close to the road and you couldn't smell them anymore when they died in the fall, past the spots where white kids cruised on weekend nights—Putt-Putt, where I'd sometimes pass the train, and McDonald's and the Triangle Drive-In—and on into town, right on by Krispy Kreme's shining green and red neon sign imperatively flashing *Hot Doughnuts NOW* as if the words meant something, and past fat-ass Lincolns and Cadillacs parked at Food Fair and at Davis Department Store over at Thruway, and past the old women who drove the Caddies and who struggled to open and close their fat-ass car doors.

Don't none of the people in this town know nothin' about nothin', I'd think, and they don't want to know nothin'. But I don't know nothin' either, and don't have nowhere to go, and don't know how to get there if I did.

Until it turned cold that fall, I'd lie in the sun and suck beer and listen to Isaac Hayes eight-tracks. I'd walk down to Silas Creek and stare at the water and try to imagine me and some girl (any girl) in rolled-up jeans splashing about just like in Salem cigarette ads. And when I went back inside, I did the old funky strut in front of the mirrors, angling my body as if I was one bad stud midnight Ali/black motherfucker. If Carol walked past while I was at the mirrors, I'd zing a couple fast jabs a half-inch from her face to run her ass off.

Around four o'clock, I'd start preening to go out. Just before time for Daddy to get home, I'd steal a few dollars from the top drawer of his bureau and leave the house. I'd buy a couple sixes of Miller Malt and maybe a Zero bar or pack of Saltines and a box of Swisher Sweets cigars for dessert, then take the Camaro up to Sherwood Forest Elementary, the school I'd been going to when my mother died, where I'd push my Stylistics tape into the player—*Betcha by golly, wow,* the disembodied voices would croon, *You're the one that I've been waiting for*—and there I'd sit in the parking lot and pretend to talk to my own personal specialprivateladyfriend, tell her all the secrets I didn't have but desperately felt I needed to talk about.

* * *

I'm on the playground. Riding the roundabout. I lay my head way back and watch clouds roll around me. I get dizzy. I look down. And she's there, naked and wet, like she stepped from a stream, and she's standing in front of the pines. Her hair flows down the sides of her face. The roundabout stops. I stare. Her skin is luminous with water and suntan and ancestry. She's standing, legs apart, hands on her hips, waiting for me. Standing like girls in Playboy. *Beads of water reflect light from the V of black hair down there. I step off the roundabout. My mouth feels numb. I run my tongue across my gums. I don't feel any teeth. I reach in: they all fall out. I see them lying in the sand. I look up. And she's gone.*

* * *

By late October I was so frustrated that I'd run down the hill, past the swings and the roundabout and the sandbox, down to the center of the baseball field, and I'd peer down at Daddy's house, nestled deep inside its noiselessness, and I'd think about him and Carol sitting there watching Andy Griffith on TV. And

I'd walk in one great circle for a time before I'd stop and, in the monochromatic light from the fat moon, I'd snatch my hat from my head and fling it out across the sand, pull heavy-starched shirt and razor-creased trousers from my body and crumple them into knots and slam them in the dust and I'd run, reed-thin white and naked, glowing ghostlike under the moon, through gray brittle frost-laden crabgrass and I'd snort the air and smoke it out in silver ice clouds and I'd smash empty beer bottles against rough pine bleachers and I'd take my left hand, curl my fingers toward my palm, squeezing my nails hard into the flesh like Sensei had taught, ball up my fist as stiff as a mace, and I'd hit myself again and again and again, on my belly, my abdomen, my legs, until I went first red then purple and I'd hit myself some more.

I wanted it to hurt, bad, but I never seemed to feel the pain and, even if I did, I still hadn't hurt myself bad enough to make me feel better, so I'd tug my trousers back on and my shirt and I'd find my cap and climb back up the hill, trying to smooth out the wrinkles as best I could. And I'd drive home and it'd be two to three in the morning and I'd sneak in the last couple beers, take a seat in the den, turn on the television, and drink and sob silently until I lost myself in the familiar steady drone of the post-sign-off test pattern.

*　*　*

Not knowing anything that I wanted, but figuring I had to do something before my father booted me out of the house, I started college on August 23, 1973. It was less than five months before my twenty-second birthday. I'd reached my full adult height, five-foot-seven, and I weighed ninety pounds. I'd never become the greatest heavyweight champion of all times, but at least I was too skinny to be sent to Vietnam. What's more, I'd finally gotten tall enough not to need a seat cushion to drive.

Eight

NOT FIVE DAYS AFTER having met Bruce Lee in *Enter the Dragon*, I found an article that had been written by the man himself, found in it a wisdom alive and new and China to me (and, beyond China, the *world!*), among molding, sweet-smelling stacks of magazines in the basement of the Lees-McRae Junior College library in Banner Elk, North Carolina, USA.

The title: "Liberate Yourself from Classical Karate."

Accompanying the article were three black-and-white photos of Lee sparring with a robot-looking type, into whose head and body were being chunked punches and kicks rocketed from impossible-seeming angles. Impossible in that I'd seen no one else who could've conceived of them, much less done them.

These photos were not movie-still glossies, but images of techniques as real as Lee's brick-hard fists: fists sheathed, in the photos, by thickly padded boxing gloves.

Lee's partner had on Everlast boxing headgear. Despite the protection, the partner's features were being contorted by the impact of Lee's blows. And once again: you could see it, even in these frozen glimpses, boiling up from Lee's insides. The Power, affecting itself in waves upon the catcher, the sparring "partner," the heavy bag with legs. Both men were working out in sweat clothes and tennis shoes. Lee wasn't wearing a shirt and he was bouncing about on the balls of his feet, like a boxer. His skin refracted southern California sun.

"Classical karate" types (Sensei and the *karateka*s I'd seen in martial arts magazines) would never have posed for photographs, or even worked out, in such attire. They would've been decked out in starched white uniforms and full black-belt drag, driving stakes through boards with their foreheads or allowing themselves to be run over by half-ton Toyota flatbeds.

I studied the pictures a long, awed time before I read the words. And was not disappointed when I got to the body of the story.

"I am concerned with the blossoming of a martial artist," Lee wrote, "not a Chinese martial artist or a Japanese martial artist. A martial artist is a human being first. As nationalities have nothing to do with one's basic humanity, so they have nothing to do with martial art.

"Leave all preconceptions behind," Lee said. "Leave your protective shell of isolation," he told me, "and relate *directly* to what is being said."

Fetus, he was calling, *come out, come out, wherever you are.*

"Fighting, as is, is simple and total," Lee continued. "It is not limited to your perspective or conditioning as a Chinese or Korean martial artist. True observation begins when one sheds set patterns, and true freedom of expression occurs when one is beyond systems. Regardless of their many colorful origins (by a wise, mysterious monk, by a special messenger in a dream, or in a holy revelation), styles are created by men. A style should not be considered gospel truth....Man, the living, creating individual, is always more important than any style."

In that moment, for the first time ever, I wasn't nothing. It no longer bothered me not to be just like other kids. For the first time I felt like something, and that something (someone!) had been named. There was nothing wrong with being different. Being different could mean being an individual. I was an *individual!* Or at least I could become one. When I began living.

"At best, styles are parts dissected from a whole. Divisive by nature, styles keep men apart rather than unite them."

Lee was referring specifically to systems of martial art—Tae Kwon Do, karate, kung fu, judo, kendo—but I took the term (and Lee's article) allegorically, to apply to any conditioning, any training, any capsulization, any categorization, any habit. "Style" could mean religiosity, ethnicity, any prejudice. It might mean lifestyle, or any other *way* of thinking or being. It could mean idealizing a person, notion, or situation; it could mean regarding one region of the world, or people who live there, as being better than another. It might mean making a big fucking deal out of Christmas or a stupid fucking football team or having to use "good" goddamn table manners or most any ol' construct. It might even mean feeling that to make it through the day you need a clean mean ride with a full tank of gas and have to wear snazzy trousers and hard-starched shirts.

Then. It began seeming like one tiny dumb joke, finally; all of it. Everything that I'd perpetrated on myself for half of my life. Wallowing in the romance of sorrow, in the joy of melancholy. Blaming my lot on my mother's death, on God, on people, on the world. I'd closed myself off to most everyone and everything around me, and to myself, although I stayed so deeply inside of me. Inside of me in unfortunate ways.

I'll not do it any longer, I declared right at that moment. I choose not to frame myself, not to encapsulate myself, not to "live" in a shell any longer. Nor will I adopt a "lifestyle," choose somebody else's way, to replace my shell. I'll not join anybody's colony; not select a side; choose neither to believe nor to disbelieve; not step along; not be a passenger.

I choose, instead, to live a life. Fetus will punch and kick his way out of his shell.

"Look around the martial arts," Lee continued, "and witness the assortment of routine performers, trick artists, desensitized robots, glorifiers of the past. *Life is constant movement—* rhythmic as well as random. Life is continual change, not stagnation. Instead of choicelessly flowing with this process of change, many 'masters,' past and present, rigidly subscribe to traditional concepts and techniques of the art, solidifying the everflowing, dissecting the totality."

Reading Bruce Lee's words, I finally saw my own Japanese/ Negroese isolationist rituals for what they were. At best, I'd chosen to "live" parts of the *LIFE* available to me, to limit my experiences, to solidify the everflowing, to choose the security of my cage, to settle for a niche, over the vast, vast world open to us.

"Lacking boundaries," Lee wrote, "combat is always fresh, alive, constantly changing. Consider the subtle difference between having no form and having no-form. The first is ignorance; the second, transcendence. Through instinctive body feeling"—*Fetus, get back to what you once were,* he was saying; *what you are*—"each of us *knows* our own most efficient

51

and dynamic manner of achieving leverage, balance in motion, economic use of energy. Patterns, techniques and forms touch only the fringe of understanding."

These were ideas (non-ideas?) I'd not previously heard. "These paragraphs are, at best, a finger pointing to the moon," Lee concluded. "Do not take the finger to be the moon or fix your gaze so intently on the finger as to miss the beautiful sights of heaven."

He'd said similar lines in *Enter*. I'd not understood them when I saw the movie. Reading "Liberate Yourself from Classical Karate," I felt that I did. I admired his presumptive nonpresumptiveness, his pretentious nonpretentiousness. But what struck me most was the implied belief that people should have a grace, a fluidity, of personality and of thought and of movement. To have less is to be not quite human, not quite alive.

Lee intimated that these properties are innate—and that we've forgotten them. Most important, his body stated in movement, these attributes can be recovered and honed. "Yes," I said aloud. A rounder, cosmic *Yes!!* roared up from my gut.

Over the next few weeks I ordered numerous back issues of martial arts magazines with articles about or by Lee, and looked up every account I could find of his death, not only at Lees-McRae but twenty miles down the Blue Ridge, in Boone, at Appalachian State University's library.

"Kung-fu movie star" was how most newspaper articles categorized him. At first I cared what they called Lee, then I quit caring what they said and quit reading their easy obits, though I was mystified by the lack of real writing about the man—this meteoric, snapshot-brief presence—his death and his *life*.

Nine

THE FIRST TIME ANYONE CALLED ME SMART, other than my father, was at Lees-McRae. The person was Karen Barefoot, my freshman composition teacher.

Like me, it was Karen's first year at Lees-McRae. Born in Charlotte, she had taught at a university in Melbourne, Australia. While there, she had written and (unsuccessfully) submitted short fiction to magazines in the United States. When she'd got the hankering to come back to North Carolina, she'd chosen Lees-McRae because, she said, "It seemed like the right environment to do serious work."

And Lees-McRae's campus did look like a "serious" place. The Old-Worldish white stone buildings seemed to have been carved from the very ribs of the mountain on which they'd been erected, and furniture in those buildings hand-hewn from ancient, wind-gnarled, reptilian-trunk cedar and hemlock forests that adorned nearby Beech and Sugar Mountains' regal bodies—forests whose rising, glowing morning mists, tinted by pigments in the needles, give the Blue Ridge chain its name. All in all, a postcard-perfect setting for a small campus.

Of course, academic-seeming cosmetics aren't why I went to

Lees-McRae. I could tell you that I chose the school because it was small (560 students) and because area ski resorts looked like places that James Bond should hang out. But the real reason I landed at "Lose-McRae," as we students called it, was that it was the only school with standards crummy enough for folks in its admissions office to give me a chance. And even then, they decided that I'd be on academic probation my first year.

In the fourteen months since high school, I'd begun to grow up and get more sophisticated. I'm sure this is true because at Lees-McRae I learned to lie better than in high school. Or at least more profitably. I became an A student, not because I was studious, but because I learned to appear bright. Which isn't tough, when you're as geeky-looking as me.

The class that I most enjoyed was Karen's. I liked it because she encouraged students to call her Karen, because she didn't mind if we didn't come to lectures "as long as you find something worthwhile to do," because she taught by telling stories, because she let us write about what we wanted (the more personal the better), and because she was a stone fox. I began to write pseudo-seriously because Karen believed that I was good at it and wasn't shy about saying so. And if it would mean pleasing Karen, well, I'd just become the greatest writer of all times.

Karen was lean and tall, and her hair was alive and dark and long. She wore it French-braided on the sides like Olivia Hussey had in a couple scenes in Franco Zeffirelli's *Romeo and Juliet,* which Karen showed in class before we read the play. Karen wore round, wire-rimmed glasses and jeans and peasant tops or thin sundresses. And as she stood in streaming shafts of sun at the front of class, reading one or another of her favorite passages from books she'd assigned, standing in filtered sunlight speaking in her slow and sultry Southern melody, it wasn't at all hard to tell that Karen wore no underwear.

In class I stared at Karen, usually forgetting to listen to what she said. But I gobbled up the books she assigned. Edith Hamilton's *Classical Mythology;* Shakespeare's *A Midsummer Night's Dream; Lord Jim; Light in August; Of Mice and Men; The Old Man and the Sea; The Great Gatsby.* The only book Karen asked us to read that I couldn't get through was *Catcher in the Rye.* Who has time to listen to some juvenile maladjust whine pointlessly for a couple hundred pages? Except somebody who wishes that the world would suffer their whine. God, there's got to be something in the world beyond pointless adolescent whining.

And Karen Barefoot showed me a bit of it: I started getting off on rhythms of good writing. After class, back in my dorm room, I could enter worlds that Karen had shown me—lands of gods, goddesses, and heroes, and of men with lives so orderly their essences could be caught on paper. The coolest line I remember Karen quoting was by the Roman playwright Terence. That old slave, born about a hundred years before Jesus, said the most amazing thing: "I am human, and nothing human is foreign to me." I wish I'd known to say the same thing about myself.

My favorite character in Karen's books was Gatsby. Ol' James Gatz was awfully slick for an Anglo-Saxon. I admired his monogrammed shirts; white, pink, and yellow linen suits; sleek fast cars; and most of the rest of his style.

It was mostly because I was pretentious enough to see some irony of Gatz's life in my own, that and the knife-on-bare-skin cold mountain autumn, that I loosened up and started wearing clothes that were a little less uptown. Not to imply that I would've gone so far as to don a pair of Levi's or a colored T-shirt or tennis shoes, or even would've left the top button of a shirt undone. And there's no way I would've taken off my thin alpaca sweaters and golf caps. I'm saying only that practical winter garb was a necessity in the mountains, and the fall of 1973 was one of the coldest on record. And that my closet at school was filled, by my father's graciousness, with corduroys and flannels in most rich bright colors of the rainbow.

In my room, I could stand in front of the little mirror over the small pine dresser in the farthest corner and toss blow after blow at the reflection in the glass—five jabs from a side-stance, pivot to the front and rivet the air with four quick *sansen-tsuki,* back to the jab and up on my toes, bounding from side to side, popping the air with blows, dancing to my left and away from the mirror, thinking of the reflected face and body as that of Frazier or Sensei, or of black-garbed Ninja assassins I'd read about in the library, or of Tom Buchanan in *Gatsby,* or of the jockish assholes I imagined going out with all the fine-looking women I was interested in. Sometimes, when I was slinging punches, I even got so worked up that I took my cigar out of my mouth and left it in an ashtray on the desk. I didn't know how to throw a right hand and didn't see much purpose for the blow, what with my well-reared snake of a left jab being so fast and deadly and all.

To impress Karen Barefoot, I wrote "autobiographical" stories about having been born in Korea during the war and having studied Tae Kwon Do from the age of five. I fashioned long, self-piteous "poems" (stolen from sappy pop songs by Bread and Dan Fogelberg) about being young, brilliant, and absolutely misunderstood by everyone around me. And I wrote about Ali. The only Bs I received from Karen were for my Ali stories. I thought that the Ali papers were the only good ones.

When I wrote about Ali and boxing and karate, I worked hard at being knowledgeable. I went to the library and looked up magazine articles about Ali and any of the martial arts and read, then reread them, slowly, carefully, then read them yet again. More than read, I *internalized* the magazine pieces and didn't care if they were sloppily written.

Another cool thing began happening, too: even though I wasn't intending to learn anything, a number of my classes became fun. And because they were fun, I found myself starting to learn.

In addition to Karen, I had one other very good teacher at Lees-McRae. Mr. Wilson, who taught Religions of the World, was lots different from frumpy, twangy-tongued old disciplinarians at Mount Tabor. Mr. Wilson was tall, thin, and probably about fifty, though he had few wrinkles. If his hair hadn't been gray, you would've thought that he was maybe thirty-five.

Every day he wore a different corduroy shirt, khaki trousers, and the same pair of always new-looking brown work boots. He spoke softly, simply, carefully, he wore his shirts open-collared, and most times, even when caught unawares, he had a slight smile and look of great discovery on his face.

About three weeks into the semester and two weeks before I found Bruce Lee, on the day that we were to review for our first exam, the one on Hinduism and Buddhism, Mr. Wilson arrived for class ten minutes late. He placed his books on the desk and said, "Before we start, I want to tell you about the Chinese idea of the Superior Man."

A wave of groans rolled about the room. Mr. Wilson chuckled. "Don't worry," he said, "you won't be responsible for it on the test."

He pulled out his chair, spun it around, straddled it, and took a seat, his arms draped over the barred back. "The Bible tells us that we're born evil," he said, "but Asian philosophers say there are no such things as good and evil. Things and people are simply what they are and can't be judged as right or wrong, good or bad."

He paused, placing his right palm under his chin, and leaned forward on the chair back, giving us a moment to consider what he'd said. "And you know what else? Taoists, Buddhists, and Confucians *all* teach that there is such a person as 'the Superior Man.' Turn to page 174 in your books, where we'll look for 'the Superior Man.'...Ah, here he is—halfway down the page, end of the third paragraph. Read the lines in quotation marks for us, will you, please, Nancy?"

Nancy Blevins's voice rose from the rear of the room: " 'The way of the Superior Man is that of an empty vessel. It is easier to carry than a full one.' "

Mr. Wilson closed his book. "Thanks, Nancy. Okay, let's begin our review."

Wow. What a mind- and gut-tease. Here was a concept I could half-relate to, my Superman fantasies not long past. After class, I skipped math, went to my room, and read the chapter on Chinese philosophies, all four pages of it, in the 409-page text. The only mention of the Superior Man was in those lines on 174, offered as an example of a Chinese proverb.

I headed for the library and, after searching for an hour, found one thin book called *Chinese Proverbial Wisdom,* the author of which was a real Chinese-sounding sort named Shapiro. The Superior Man was mentioned twice:

MEDITATION 42:
The Superior Man is as water—
reach for him, he cannot be held.

MEDITATION 58:
The Superior Man
when he walks alone
is without fear.
If he must renounce society
it does not matter.

I left the library feeling perplexed *and* kind of excited.

Ten

I READ REVIEWS of *Enter the Dragon* and was surprised that most were favorable. "Bruce Lee's performance is fascinating," the reviewer for *Time* magazine wrote. "Lee died recently in Hong Kong under mysterious circumstances. He could not be more alive than here."

I wrote my own *Enter* review for the *Fountainhead*, Lees-McRae's student newspaper. I can't pretend that my piece was good; editors would've taken most anything to fill space with student copy. The paper typically used Associated Press stuff for filler.

I began shadowboxing regularly, late at night, in the hall outside my room. I concentrated on lateral movement (not easy to do in a hallway) and on throwing quick, relaxed kicks, not having learned to kick even moderately well from fat Sensei, who could barely raise a foot above knee height. I began popping kicks loose and snappy and soon found a freedom accompanying each one thrown.

"Hey, when you gonna make that movie?" guys kidded when I was out in the hall flicking kicks. "*Enter the Fetus,* right?" And they'd chuckle. "Or is it *The Fetal Connection*?" they'd kid, parodying the title of another Lee movie, *The Chi-*

nese Connection. And I'd startle myself by laughing. Because it was funny. A lot of things had recently become funny.

*   *   *

Dancing in front of the mirror in my room. Listening to the Marvin Gaye tune *Distant Lover.* Wanting to be as fluid in movement as Gaye's voice.

Wrapping the melody around me. Trying to become the song, thinking I might learn a little about what it would be to have a distant lover. Emulating the *Soul Train* dancers, I can perform most all of their moves and even work basic karate techniques into my dance, creating a couple movements I can call my own.

While dancing, working to throw a front-kick while moving laterally, not like the "kick" on page eleven of Masutaku Oyama's *Best Karate,* with which Oyama claims to have killed eight-hundred-pound bulls; Oyama's technique is slow, stiff, predictable, more push than kick, and altogether impractical.

My left pant leg slaps against itself as I bring my kick alive, throwing it slick and slippery. *Ftwuu* is the sound the kick makes as it comes in combinations—up from the floor and out to waist height, chest height, head height; head, chest, waist, groin. Fifty times, one hundred, two hundred times, on the beat, the half-beat, the quarter-beat.

*   *   *

At midterm, I had As in Mr. Wilson's and in Karen's classes, in biology, and in Western Civ, the first "good" grades I'd made since my mother had died, though I didn't much care what my grades were. I'd learned from Lee not only not to care about grades, but to not-care about them in a brand-new (non-) way. I didn't study or take notes. I simply listened carefully to what instructors said and thought about what the words meant. I was beginning to have confidence in my brightness, having been helped by Lee to recognize that I wasn't stupid—and that lots of other "stupid" people aren't, either. I'd affected that pose, that "form," in high school in the hope of becoming popular.

I dropped algebra in mid-October; the stuff didn't strike me as any more practical than Sensei's stupid strikes and stances. Why weren't we shown how to count change, how to add and subtract without using pen and paper, compute our gas mileage, do income taxes, how to cleanly, beautifully snap a left jab, say "Please" and "Thank you" and "Yes, sir" and "No, ma'am," or something, anything, we might be able to use at some point in our lives? All this robot-math stuff could use a dose of Bruce Lee real-world revamping.

At the beginning of the ten-day midterm break, when other guys drove to Florida or Myrtle Beach in groups, I drove the eighty-nine miles to my father's house alone. This was nothing new: out of pure boredom, I'd driven to Winston-Salem every weekend but one.

Fall-break week, I lurked around bars frequented by Wake Forest University kids. I'd do one or two beers, then watch around me. Most girls wore makeup that made them look oh so young and far too old. I wasn't sure whether they'd done it on purpose or if it was something they didn't realize they'd done. Few looked happy or even as if they were enjoying themselves, though a lot of them carried themselves as though they kind of thought they might be. It was weird, the way you could watch them down alcohol and see a sheen appear around them, as if they were staring at you from the other side of pieces of smoked glass, then they'd get all rubbery-looking, head to toe. It was sad, the way they tried to keep big, wet-looking smiles plastered across cosmetically enhanced features when they felt that they were being watched. Until they got real rubbery. Then they didn't care anymore. Or at least their bodies didn't.

When the bars closed, I'd drive home, sit in my room, and eat a one-pound bag of Wise potato chips or half a box of Divinity cookies. During the days I'd lie about the house, sleeping as late as I could force myself. When I woke, I'd read *The Norton Anthology of Oriental Masterpieces,* which I'd bought at the Wake Forest bookstore my first day home. After gnawing at a few pages, I'd make myself sleep an hour or two more—storing up energy, I told myself.

When I couldn't stand bed or room or sleep any longer, I'd shuffle to the kitchen, pour a glass of iced tea, and, even though my sister had sweetened the tea when she'd steeped it, I'd dump in a few more fat spoons of sugar. I'd lie on the sofa in the den, sip the golden sugar water, and stare at reruns of *Get Smart* until Daddy came home from work and he and Carol fixed supper. Then I'd lock myself in my room, pop a James Brown eight-track into the player, and begin a two-hour session of heavy-duty pimping-up before hitting the bars.

*   *   *

I'm standing in front of the mirror in white cotton briefs. *He's tall, at least seven-five. He's glaring down at me and His eyes are yellow. His face is a mass of old scar tissue. Maybe He was*

63

burned, I'm thinking. Then I see that His skin isn't white or black; it's gray. And He's not a man at all; His face is the only part made of flesh. From the shoulders down, He's a granite wall, literally. A wall that learned to walk, a wall shaped like a man.

We're going to fight, and I don't want to, but I sure ain't gonna let Him get off first. I zing Him with an eight-punch combination: straight-as-a-spear right lead to the heart; double right uppercut to His granite balls; triple hook—to the stone ribs, to the throat, one while leaping to His temple; another straight right, the punch thrown as fast as a jab; a final sing-in-the-wind hook.

I raise my arms over my head, Ali-style, in victory. I thumb my nose at my fallen opponent as Bruce did in Enter the Dragon. Twenty thousand fans in the Garden explode into applause.

Daddy steps into the room, moving through the cheering throng, sidestepping New York's finest, hopping through the ropes. He drops three pairs of clean black socks on my bed. "Put these in your drawers, Dave," he says.

Eleven

OCTOBER, NOVEMBER, DECEMBER—researching, reading, thinking. Going for walks around the lake beside my dorm, where I watch the flapping of wings above water, and through boulder-encrusted woods, where I listen to the earth move, feeling it rotate inside me. I stop smoking stogies and drinking beer, almost without noticing that I'd quit, having lost interest in S&M.

"Could I?" I regularly ask myself on those walks. "Am I?" I quiz, studying the reflection in the bathroom mirrors. "Will I?" I want to know, standing at the end of the hallway, peering out the window late at night.

By the first week of December I arrive at "Where to start?"

Twelve

WHERE HAD LEE BEGUN? Maybe by leaving the University of Washington his junior year, his interests apart from any major.

So were mine. I'd never get a degree in Lee and Ali Studies, or in Limitless Martial Art. It was time to become serious (and playful), for Fetus to break out of the bag of waters. I couldn't see how I'd do that at Lose-McRae. Guys in the dorm, sitting around punching each other's arms, ragging on each other, laughing at each other's pain. Things they felt were important, I couldn't stand it. Pussy, food, dope, money, accounting; my dick's bigger'n yours. I mean, some of this stuff matters to me, too, but Lee had shown me a larger reality.

Their chief concerns seemed to include whether to order thin 'n' crispy or thick 'n' chewy pizzas, *I was weighing whether or not to commit my life to the ways (non-ways) of the warrior;* the present football season, *I would be the finest, most complete artist that I could;* sliding down to the package store for a case of beer, *In the night, my skin would look wet with its light;* how and where to get some nookie on Saturday night, *The elegance of the elk would be mine;* where to buy answers to Mr. Hall's

Monday-morning calculus exam, *as would the speed of the cheetah;* which girls would've looked better with bigger tits or smaller asses, *the grace of the impala, the deadliness of the black mamba;* whether salaries were higher for those who'd majored in business or computer science, *and the explosiveness of a porpoise bursting into sky from out of the depths.*

No, I didn't see how I could stay a winter at Lose-McRae. The mountains were too damn cold already. I was tired of waking to ice-covered trees and frozen roads. I'd had enough cold, enough winter, enough death.

I'd "lived" death and witnessed a few of its faces. And had come to believe that there might be nothing in life but death, death itself being nothing, the nothing that keeps you from moving: *nichts, nada, niente, nihil, rien, sah mahng.*

Ali's was a vibrancy and rhythm only he could tap. Lee's was unusual, too, but he'd given indications of a life that could be mine. And I'd seen other intimations of life. In music, certainly, there *can* be life. There's death in music, too. That plaintive stuff you hear as fat-ass congregations of white folks sorrowfully and obligingly sing of Christ bringing them alive. Maybe Jesus had something going (lots of people do). But, Christ, how can any sane person take *anybody's followers* seriously? If taking them seriously ain't death, I don't know what is.

Yet I've heard, and felt, life in music. And I can't wait to listen, to investigate, further. I've felt life in dance, too: it's in the doing, in the moving with what is.

In writing? Yes, there's life in the act of writing. But one can appear to gain understanding through reading without knowing

a damn thing. And reading many times brings sleep. Also, whatever you read is never as big as the experience it's about—and it's
always in the past; it's dead. But writing is immediate, it's happening now, there's movement in writing, even if many writers
are deathmongers. "We are scabs and open wounds," claims old
dead Chaucer. Donkey poop. If we're scabs, we're scabs that
sing! Or at least we try to.

Where else might I find life? In family? In home? I don't know.
So much of our notion of family life seems a well-intentioned,
big-askew dream. How many family "holiday celebrations"
have you seen where folks aren't aching and/or sleeping, just
waiting for the damn turkey to get skeletonized so they can get
the fuck out of Aunt Myrtle's and on with their lives? Well,
maybe you've seen one or two, I can't say, but this boy sure
hasn't. It's almost all artifice. How can real celebration take
place on appointed times, appointed days? Too much form, too
much robotics for me.

Can I find life through another person? A woman? What about
love, that most prostituted of words? Can there be life in love? It
can't be true when we say we've *fallen* in love; love is something
you grow in. People whine in pop songs about how they'd like
to drown in a sea of love. I'd rather swim than sink. It may be
possible to find life in love, but not in the Hallmarkcard/
popsongsappy way.

Yet. Right now. Right here. I know enough to begin.

Something, this thing that even when I was eleven years old
a bit of me felt would happen, is happening, if I'll allow it. Why
folks settle for something other than this something, I can't say.

Children know that their parents are afraid to be alive. At least I thought *I* knew it.

But it doesn't matter. I'm certain that there can be life, and I'll be in it. I'll not settle for death, or for death posing as life.

Exams were coming up and that would be it, Lose-McRae would be gone, bye-bye, dead as history. I didn't know what I'd do for money (find a job; grow up, son), but I had to find out if I could fight, I had to write about martial art and Ali and Lee, and organized school was not the place to be. What I needed to know, I'd not learn between the walls of any institution.

Lee had shown me that institutions were other façades behind which death lurked.

Thirteen

FOR THREE MONTHS I'd been poring over daily newspapers in the library, hoping to spot a Lee movie playing somewhere. This Thursday was the day. LITTLE DRAGON LI LIVES, Baby Ruth–style letters proclaimed.

Above this proclamation was a series of ideograms I took to mean the same thing. Below, movie titles were listed in the language that I knew. Not just one, but all three of Lee's Hong Kong pictures: *The Big Boss*, *Fist of Fury*, and *Way of the Dragon*. It was a Bruce Lee festival! The name of the theater offering the tribute was the American, on the Bowery in New York's Chinatown. "A special two-week engagement—Starting Today!"

"This may be your last chance to see Bruce's fast as winds kick. His two legs sing quick as three in heroic action. Also, Free Gift! A smart Bruce photo for you."

The newspaper was six days old. I hurried to my room and packed a change of clothes. I had $114.17 in the bank, the remainder of my allowance for the semester. In Boone I filled the Camaro with 24.9-cents-per-gallon premium, ran it through a car wash, and was on my way, off and ready to take a chomp out of the Huge Ol' Apple.

I drove straight through the night, stopping to fuel up, chow down, piss, and stretch. I tooled the Camaro into Manhattan through the Lincoln Tunnel. It was Friday morning at eight. I saw more people in half an hour than I'd seen in my whole life. Frozen in traffic, I watched a sad-looking woman in her forties walk up the street in an expensive purple dress and coat, high-heeled purple shoes, and purple beehive hairstyle, walking her purple poodle on a purple, rhinestone-studded leash. Two police cars played bumper tag at fifteen miles an hour. The chrome and steel made crunching noises, the policemen's heads were tossed sharply forward, they creaked the cars apart, threw their heads back in openmouthed, drunken laughter—then conjugated the automobiles again and laughed some more. I had no reason to believe that they'd been drinking.

I saw cabbies scream yellow *watchoutI'mcoming!* vehicles through red lights at somewhere near fifty miles an hour, without apparently looking in either direction, finding openings where there seemed to be none. (Talk about masters!) I watched another policeman's billy club thump a passed-out man on the head in front of Madison Square Garden. I saw a man in an eighth-floor window shoot a BB rifle at passersby while yet another policeman watched and shook his head and laughed. I watched a nattily dressed old man shuffle up the street with an empty grocery bag all the way down over his head. Then I drove back to New Jersey, where I took a room at a Howard Johnson's.

Midafternoon I glided into the dank, dark world of a packed Chinatown movie house. *Where have all these people come from at this time of day?* The crowd was screaming, clapping, laughing. I sat as still as I could and studied the full Bruce Lee saga. Only one of the movies was subtitled. All three were in Chinese. I couldn't understand a word, of course, but felt that I got what Lee was saying, anyway.

After the third and best movie, *Way of the Dragon,* I left Chinatown and New York and drove straight to the Howard Johnson's, where I slept a couple hours, too fired up to stay in bed, grabbed whole-wheat toast and juice—no more doughnuts and sodas for this kid!—and started down I-95 to bigger better beautiful Banner Elk, having seen the sights I wanted to see.

Fourteen

I'M NOT AFRAID *of them. Not anymore. They've hurt old people and children and women and animals and the world and wimps and themselves. I'll not be hurt again.*

Ignorance lies heavy on their tongues. Films of sleep cloud their eyes. Arfmann and King Mobeley; Romo and Weso, too. I stand before them. My body glows ripe with the rainbow hovering around me, the rainbow my fear creates.

And they come. I feel yellow and orange break from one end of the spectrum and spring as beams from my fingertips. Vermilion jets ease quickly off my toes. And they bow: Romo and Arfmann and Sam Stone. They fall: Richard J. Reynolds and Tom Buchanan and careless ol' shithead Daisy. Where they bow, there they fall and they look up to me. Their eyes have come alive. I reach to them, help them to their feet. They smile and understand. So do I. And I wake, happy.

* * *

It was an unusually warm afternoon for December. High in the mid-fifties. I walked from Avery Dorm over to Wildcat Lake, watched and listened to waves lap non-music against the shore.

I kicked off shoes, socks, felt ground beneath my feet. God, it felt good.

Hell, yes, I'd do it.

I'd get clean and dirty. The two aren't separate. I'd bathe in dreams and in lightning.

Images of fresh green and yellow vegetables, crisp red and orange fruits, and a life beyond cynicism flashed behind my eyes. I tried to imagine catching a sanctified buzz from a tall, cold glass of water.

I closed my eyes, took my first real breath of real air in years. Opened them, took another slow one, and smiled. I was going to do good stuff; more than that, I'd *be* good stuff.

Packed books and clothes, pulled the Ali poster and Lee pictures from the wall, and left a handwritten copy of a Zen koan on the mattress, the one I'd read in my religions-of-the-world book, about how to remove a live goose from a thin-necked bottle without harming the bird or the container:

There, it's out!

Loaded the trunk and backseat of the Camaro, filled up with gas, slid Stevie Wonder's *Inner Visions* into the tape deck, and started toward home. Exams? What exams? Late-afternoon sun felt fine filtering through tinted windows. I was as awake as a pen-kept dog about to be set loose in the woods. Halfway to Boone, I rolled down the window and smilingly tossed my Ben Hogan cap up and out into the emptiness.

Made a stop at a sporting goods store in Boone. Trotting to the Camaro in the first sweatsuit and running shoes I'd owned—and minus the remainder of my Lose-McRae allowance—I felt great. My life had begun.

Section Two

A NEW LIFE

Is not the flute that soothes
the very one that was cut from wood with knives?

—KAHLIL GIBRAN

Fifteen

I'M IN DR. BUTLER'S OFFICE, my father's doc who looks like that asshole Jesse Helms. Despite this liability, Dr. Butler's a nice guy. My whole life, I've seen Dr. B. when I've been out and around with Daddy, but I've never been to him as a patient. I've always visited my pediatrician, Dr. Glenn. At almost twenty-two, this is my first visit to a grown-up's doc.

Dr. Butler pokes, prods, and thumps on me here, there, and most everywhere, then gives his okay to begin training. "But," he says, wagging his finger at me, "you'd better start light."

I laugh out loud. Not at Dr. Butler—but at me. My puny little body would implode on the spot if I even dreamed of starting "heavy."

Tugging down my T-shirt after Dr. B. has listened to my heart, I ask if the big chocolate-colored birthmark on the right side of my chest means anything. "I reckon it's something you'll have to live with, son," he says, chuckling. Then, "It's nothing to worry about," he assures me. "You know, though...here's something interesting on the X ray. Anybody ever tell you, you have an extra rib?" He pats what I hope will become my well-packed right pectoral muscles. "Right about here—under all that excess pigment."

He laughs again and turns toward the door. "Guess that means there's no woman for you."

It's a joke I don't understand. Looking over his shoulder, he sees I'm puzzled. "Don't you read your Bible, son? Woman was created from one of man's ribs."

I laugh out of politeness, but later, at home, looking at my chest in the mirror, I begin to worry about the awful possibility. No woman for me.

*   *   *

Standing in the bathroom late at night, staring in the mirror once again. Well, what d'ya know? Funny I've never noticed. The birthmark on my chest is the same shape as that of mainland China.

Sixteen

I START MY LEE-INSPIRED WORKOUTS the second week of January 1974, just before my birthday. On Daddy's bathroom scales I weigh in at ninety-two pounds. Push though I may (and I do), I'm unable to perform a single push-up. I try them stooped on all fours, what we called "women's push-ups" in high-school gym class.

When I've worn myself out on a (very) few of these, I run twice around my father's half-acre backyard, my legs stiff, tripping in mole holes and almost falling. I finish my day with ten overhead presses with the twenty-two-pound, baby-blue plastic weight set Daddy'd tried to motivate me with when he'd bought it for me the year after my mother had passed. The next morning I'm so sore I can hardly lift my arms over my head.

All through the winter and spring I stay with my workouts, and soon I'm able to run five times around the yard—then ten, fifteen, twenty. I dig deep every day, and after a few months I sprint the last five laps and bound down the creekbank, through the water, and up the other side, and I churn through the woods and briars, then follow the creek all the way down to Shaffner Park and back, creating my own ambling four-mile path.

By then I'm squeezing out push-ups in multiples: three sets of ten, twenty, then thirty-five, now fifty; eventually I get up to grinding out more than five hundred a day.

In January I started with five sit-ups per workout; one year later, I'm at one thousand, six days a week, every single week. Add a couple hundred crunches and leg raises on top of that. Like Lee, I teach myself to do push-ups on my fingertips; and on the thumb and forefinger of each hand; and even, eventually, to perform one-arm push-ups.

Eating four overflowing multi-plate meals every sixteen hours, then adding a gallon of whole milk and a couple blenders of ground-up ice cream, bananas, and Bob Hoffman's quick-weight-gain powder (a variation of what I'd learned Lee himself had done to gain weight), I force the bathroom scales to 105, then 112, 119, 121.

I remember walking past the mirror in just a pair of gym shorts and spotting a muscular torso out of the corner of my left eye: crisply defined pecs, trapezius, lats, deltoids, everything. For part of a second, I wonder who this person is in the mirror. Then I smile...though I'm still not sure this is *my* image.

I order a blue vinyl punching bag from an advertisement in a karate magazine, and when it comes, I pack it with rags and a couple worn-out pillows. I shove fists and feet into its man-made hide day after day, night after night. After several months I purchase an Everlast prepacked ninety-pound black leather bag from Bocock-Stroud's Sporting Supplies, and empty the stuffings from my blue vinyl critter into a garbage can, refilling its flattened husk with more than a hundred hard pounds of sand from the creek behind Daddy's.

For my twenty-second birthday, Daddy'd bought me a wooden-handled, fine leather jump rope. Lee's the only martial practitioner I've seen (either in a magazine or in person) who jumps rope. I feel that I have something up on most other karate dorks because I've watched Ali work with ropes. At first I step on the rope and trip over it and hurt my ankles and shins and calves and almost fall with every turn. I bend my knees, too, instead of holding them straight, and use my arms when I should turn it only with wrists. But I'm not embarrassed not to know what I'm doing. In fact, I'm surprised I'm not self-conscious about much of anything I'm trying, even if it is amazing how quick the rope gets me tired and I find myself gasping and wheezing like an emphysema victim.

But eventually I sure do get good with that thang. The day comes when I can tap into a big bunch of different rhythms and scramble them all up in almost any order I want: jump with a skipping stutter-step one leg at a time; move laterally across the room; backward and forward, up and down the floor; whip the rope beneath my feet two turns for every time I jump; even jump like film I've seen of "Sugar" Ray Robinson hobbling around in a full squat, looking like some huge crustacean.

I become entranced by the wondrously soothing *and* stimulating sounds of my rope slapping concrete and of a well-worked speed bag bouncing back and forth on its wooden platform. I hang an Everlast 4204 Turbo over in the corner and commune with the small bag's shining leather bladder for close to half an hour per workout.

And, by my standards, I'm becoming A BIG, STRONG, HUMONGOUS, GIANT SUMGUN. Within a couple years I'm up to ten consecutive three-minute rounds on the rope and on each of three heavy bags—the Everlast for punches, kicks, knees, and elbows; the one filled with sand for open-hand blows; the third and lightest one for high kicks—a far greater number of rounds than most world-champion boxers would do preparing for fights.

Day after day, month after month, I go down to the basement to dance with my Everlast. It's always there, hanging sure and straight and silent in the center of the room, seeming to fill most of the 1,500-square-foot space. I rip into the bag with hands and feet, concentrating on speed—Ali speed, Bruce Lee speed, godly speed, my speed—quickly discovering that the more relaxed I am, the faster, more powerful, and more precise techniques become. I eventually get to where I can zing four, six, even eight shots per second. By this time I recognize that I'm maybe the second or third fastest human I've ever seen.

As I work the Everlast, I sometimes finish rounds with a step-across side-kick. When I pump the side-kick well, it bends the big bag nearly in two and swings it up and away, toward thick cedar beams creaking in the ceiling. At the top of its flight it seems to hang, and just when there's cause to wonder if Newton's Laws have been suspended, it starts to fall—a steam-driven piston that lands with a bright, concussive *Claung!* and a jerk that shakes dust and splinters from the rafters and plaster from the walls.

I become enraptured not only with the heft of the Everlast and its reliability, but with the feel of sweat on my skin. I get to where I can't stand to wear unnecessary clothes—and come to think of most shirts and trousers as just that: not needed.

The judge does not agree. During my second summer of training, I receive a traffic citation for driving without having my license with me. (I'd stopped carrying a wallet, not wanting to be burdened with it; it limited my freedom of movement.) As the ticket is being written, I'm told by the arresting officer that if I bring my license to court, the charges will probably be dropped. On the appointed morning, I go for an early run, then tool down to the courthouse with my license—barefoot, shirtless, wearing only a pair of workout shorts. As the flattop-sporting judge enters the chambers, he spies me, seated in the gallery. He points and frowns, then waves me forward. I rise calmly from my seat and amble over to the well-polished mahogany guardrail, glowingly confident of my own rightness. "I'll give you twenty minutes to find yourself some clothes," he says, short and hard. For the life of me, I don't understand why he's upset. But I leave, to return wearing T-shirt and shoes.

*   *   *

First thing each morning and fifteen minutes before bed every night, I perform upper- and lower-body stretches. I find a short, square, Japanese-style table in an import shop, which I buy, along with a green clay garden Buddha. I place the Buddha at the rear of the table, an incense burner in its lap, and line up five small candles near the front of the table. Every night, after my evening stretches, I light the candles, turn off the lights, and sit naked before the Buddha, meditating while listening to my Marvelous Marvin Gaye record, *Let's Get It On.* On the way to bed, I snuff out all five candles with a series of air-popping kicks and punches.

I buy a full-length mirror that I place against a wall in the basement, and spend an hour a day shadowboxing in front of it; half an hour of free-form punching: jab, jab, jabjabjab, back-fist, more jabs, different style jabs, switch sides and jab with the right, different back-fists, left hooks, a whipping motion on the end of some jabs to approximate the power of a hook, overhand rights, right leads; then a second half-hour making the air snap and pop with kick combinations—front-kick, side-kick; round-kick, hook-kick, side-kick; crescent kick, spinning reverse crescent kick, round-kick. All of it feels so fine and liberating that I actually begin to wonder if I might be able to teach myself to fly.

After thirty minutes of punching and another thirty of kicks, I combine kicks, punches, and hand-strikes for a few rounds. As I throw techniques, I suck air in deep and blow it out hard, giving myself, in effect, a continual series of Zen slaps, seeking to constantly wake myself. Popping the air with blows too fast to count, I imagine lightning coursing through my limbs. Always patterning my style on what I've seen Lee do in the movies and on Ali's boxing (as well as on what feels glowingly natural), I find rhythms and a suppleness that I feel have been asleep inside me. My Lee-inspired workouts also help me feel, for the first time ever, that I'm not a fraud—that, indeed, I'm one very real slice.

And, as I'll discover years later, as is true of the very best sex, (many) moments occur in which you know that you're not the one doing the moving, but that you're living inside the movement. And I learn something else fundamental: there ain't nothin' a human being can do, no matter how impossible it may at first seem, that another one can't do, too.

*   *   *

Someone's standing in front of me. He's naked. His lean golden torso refracts light, breaks it gently and it wavers near him in prisms. At first I don't know this man. Then I see that he's me. Only I'm unashamed of my nakedness. And my face has sprouted a thick, glowing beard that I know, even in the dream, I can't grow. I'm playing a flute. Not with mouth or hands. The pipe is part of my body. The instrument plays itself.

*   *   *

I apply for a job at the convenience store where I used to buy beer and I know the manager on a first-name basis. Jim hires me to work second shift, which allows me to support my martial addiction—not only by giving me a few dollars—but also because, when I'm in the store by myself, I get to read all the martial-arts and boxing rags on the magazine rack. We sell a few paperbacks in the store, too, and I buy a copy of Norman Mailer's *The Fight,* which blows me completely away. It's the first *real* writing I've encountered about Ali and about the science of boxing; I had no idea something I was passionate about could be presented in such an accessible way—without destroying its power and mystery. Indeed, for me, Mailer enhances the mysteries of pugilism by beautifully exploring them.

Between customers, in addition to reading, I do push-ups, stretch, a little shadow; think up, work on, and polish combinations until they gleam. It's the first job I've had. I'm surprised how much I enjoy it.

I recall getting in from work one 1974 midnight and spooning out a few vegetables Daddy had left simmering on the stove, then carrying my plate into the den. While I stand with the plate in my right hand, forking stewed carrots into my mouth with the left, watching Johnny Carson while standing barefoot on the carpet, I throw three—count 'em, THREE— whippingly wonderful and beatifically beautiful round-kicks, all without touching my foot to the floor, cleanly snapping the heads from all three porcelain Cupid statuettes who are sitting there minding their own business on a bookshelf high up over to the left side of the TV.

I'm not upset by this (after all, consider the control it took to perform this wondrous feat); rather, I'm amazed—"Hey, wow, cool," I must've said—then, when I finish my final meal of the day and reach some level of post-martial sobriety, I try to repair my dead mom's old figurines with Elmer's wood glue.

When I'm not working out or pulling time at the convenience store, I'm studying Lee and Ali, sometimes in movie houses, sometimes on TV, and, most often, in free movies that roll behind my eyes. And I'm devouring all the Lee and Ali magazines, as well as every book and periodical about martial art and boxing, that I can find. After studying *The Fight* again and again, my interest in real writing, in literary storytelling, keeps growing. I reread the novels from Karen's class at Lees-McRae and ask clerks in bookstores what fiction they enjoy most. I find more and more good nonfiction writers that way, too: Tim O'Brien, Harry Crews, Tom Wolfe, Joan Didion, Maxine Hong Kingston, all of whom open me further and further to the possibilities of the world of storytelling. And as I continue to grow, the world keeps getting bigger and bigger.

And then. I'm at 123, and 26, 28, 31, 35, and 140 (the same weight Lee had been most of his adult years). What keeps me fascinated with Lee and with martial art itself, day in and day out, is the belief that I'm doing something—shine on, shine on—and, even more powerfully, I have the sense that in every moment there's something extraordinary to learn, some lush place to go that is throbbingly, achingly remarkable.

*   *   *

I'm alone in a small, mirrored room, sitting in the middle of the wooden floor, relaxing and listening to my body hum as it cools. I slowly stand, step to the mirrors, and leap into a jumping, spinning crescent kick. When I should plop down to the floor, I keep levitating up. I cross my legs, close my eyes, sit on the air, and float. I know entirely, exactly what I am doing; I am in absolute control. I sense someone at the door and glide to the floor, remaining in a full lotus. One of my students enters the room and asks if I've been training.

"I've just finished," I say, and then I wake, happy and laughing, full of my body-buzz, filled with the power of the dream, full of belief in the dream, and with the knowledge that, yes, I can do it—I can fly.

Seventeen

I⟨T'S A BRIGHT⟩, cold, windy morning in April 1976. Tuesday, my day off from the store. I'm running five miles on the path behind my father's house. Sunlight flashes through tender green shoots that have sprung from overhanging branches of willows. I don't feel the cold on my skin, only in my lungs, where it burns as it rushes in with each breath: two steps—breathe in through nose and mouth; two more—out with a whoosh, unbelievably grateful to be able to release warm, wet steam-clouds back into the day, feeling the thawing loam under my Pumas.

Dallas is running with me and he's a welcome partner. After all, he's the only guy I know who doesn't think I'm nuts for running not only forwards, but backwards, sideways, and cross-legged, skipping, leaping into forward rolls and tossing jabs, hooks, and uppercuts at tree limbs and launching round-kicks and flying side-kicks at every telephone pole we pass.

But some folks think Dallas isn't normal, either. Hell, Dallas doesn't even look like your average pooch. In some ways he more resembles a cow than a canine. His daddy was dalmatian, his mama English bull, and since he's the one puppy in his litter that lived, that makes him, to the best of my knowledge, the world's first and only bullmatian. He has a dalmatian's long legs, speed, spots, playfulness, and stinky-ass skin; and he inherited his mama's good looks—the squashed Joe Frazier face (and fighting skill), a twenty-five-inch neck, and Arnold Schwarzenegger shoulders and chest. Some people think Dallas is ugly. I think Dallas is almost as pretty as me.

As we push through the wind and bound past the house, Dad steps out the back door to leave for work. He yells, "Look out for your sister, Dave." I wave and shift concentration back to my run, losing myself to my body's sweet, warm songs.

That evening, when Dad gets in from work, I've just picked myself up from the cocoonlike impression I've made in the carpet in front of the TV, after completing a few hundred sits and pushes. My back is turned to the door and I'm in the farthest corner of the den, slinging combinations at squat-bodied samurai as they erupt from under the floors, jump down from the ceiling, spring out from behind walls. The wind makes the windows howl and squeak and moan. I bob and weave under a waist-wide sword being swung by a short, fast, hard, little man, slide to the right, front-kick up through his intra-articular fat pad into the backside of his left knee. He drops his weapon as he's slammed against the wall.

I feel Dad behind me before he says, "Hello, son."

I turn to greet him, glad he's home early. But I'm at the height of my shadow-fighting fantasy; I'm pumped up big-time. I wheel toward him and smile, big and loose. "Pops," I say, "check this out."

I jet a couple quick shots toward his face, maybe a quarter of an inch away, just playing in a serious way, having fun.

"Stop, son," he says, startled, backing up.

"Relax," I say, chuckling at his insecurity, not seeing how tired he is. "I ain't gonna hit you."

He leans toward me a little. The next technique I throw catches him flush on his left cheek, under the eye. It's a close-fisted shot that explodes into his face. His head snaps back and to my left. Unlike the guys Lee pounds on in the movies, Dad's face doesn't go bright with the thrill of pain. And he doesn't smilingly accept a fistic lesson like the volunteers I've playfully moved with in gyms and dojangs. Instead, as the color flows from his cheeks, my father looks sick and very old. Utterly reduced.

He bites down hard on his lower lip, turns, and walks to his room, closing the door. I don't know what to say or do. For minutes and minutes, I stand right where I am, on almost exactly the spot where I punched him.

After a long while I work up the nerve to knock on his door; he doesn't answer. I go out to the Camaro and simply sit in the car, listening to music.

My father never says a word to me about hitting him. And I don't say anything to him. But I'm never that careless with my tools again.

Over the next few weeks, the swelling under Dad's eye washes away from purple and brown to yellow, then disappears. But the bruise is still there. Both in him and in me.

Eighteen

IF PUNCHING MY FATHER IN THE EYE is among the worst things that happened because of my years of living life at the end of fists, here are a few of the best:

1

I've driven to Greenville, North Carolina, to visit my friend Tony Lopez. We're showing his students how to cut off the ring, a skill useful to competitive fighters and to folks accosted in alleys.

I have hands up beside my head and chin tucked in next to my shoulder. With forearms, then palms, Tony shoves me into a corner and shows how to wondrously dig palms and fists into biceps to bring hands down, when to beautifully shovel fingers and elbows into spaces between ribs near the heart, how to majestically thrust knees, shins, and feet into kidneys/groin/ bladder. In this otherwise ordinary moment, I recognize the arc of my life.

Through Tony's appendages, and my own, I'm part of a big family. Our kin includes every person who has had ten-ounce sheaths of cows' hide grow onto the ends of his arms. It includes everyone who has felt music in the hypnotically repetitive *futada-futada* sound of a properly worked speed bag and who understands the relationship between this call and a rhythm inside himself.

World super-lightweight kickboxing champion Tony "Huracan" Lopez is the best-rounded martial artist I've known, and the closest person I've seen to Bruce Lee incarnate—Tony is one of the very best fighters and weapons and forms competitors in the world, and the only guy who has ever been world-ranked in each of these categories. As such, he's more than good enough to have kicked around Jhoon Rhee, with whom he studied. Rhee, credited with bringing Tae Kwon Do to America and one of Bruce Lee's best friends, took from and gave to Li Siu Loong himself. Lee studied under Yip Man, "the Gentle Whirlwind," who escaped from mainland China in 1949 and carried to Hong Kong the gung-fu style called *wing chun.* From Shaolin nun Yim Wing Chun, "the Daughter of Beautiful Springtime," to monks in her monastery, and finally to old Bodhidharma, the Indian sage reputed to have brought Buddhism and the fighting arts to China, I'm related to them all.

Our relationship is kinetic. Bruce Lee and Tony Lopez and I. Probably even old Bodhidharma.

Warriors and healers, monks and lovers, creatures of flesh and of spirit. We are hard and soft, fast yet careful, strong yet graceful. Snow clouds, fog, wind, thunder, blue skies in February and in August, drizzle, monsoons, hurricanes; there is power and beauty in all weather.

2

Early Saturday morning. I'm on my way back to Dad's from a run up to Reynolda Gardens, where Silas Creek begins. Walking home beside the creek, I watch insects as they crawl through grass, waves created by the wind on a puddle, a mockingbird as it springs from tree to tree—singing a different song on every branch, the color of a pretty girl's shoes, doors as they open and close behind me. The waters are calm; I'm the moon on the stream, *nagare sausa.*

3

Practicing hundreds of techniques and skills, I learn lots about the human body, the ways that it moves and the precise coordination of these movements required to tell a good martial story. And I'm proud of who I become. There's no way Lee himself could've worked more diligently; I push myself hard nearly every waking hour.

Eventually, I work up courage to gunsling my way into numerous karate academies in western North Carolina. I'm surprised how easy it is to chump most of the black belts in most schools (as easy and as sad as punching puppies, who don't know how to hit you back). Everywhere I go, I befuddle and dazzle thoroughly outclassed sparring partners. My intent is not to hurt people with whom I spar, *never* to hurt them, but simply to be with them. Again and again, I become bored by their skill level, and after I quit showing off, I work to bring them out, to help them engage with me. (It is the same thing I'd eventually learn to do as a prospective writer—to engage.) My talents are so much more developed than everybody's I encounter that I start to wonder if I might not become, might even already be, one of the baddest humans alive.

It is, thank goodness, a short-lived fantasy, the death of which allows me to become a much better person. Despite my well-worked, hard-fought skills, I'm eventually taught (usually kindly, sometimes tenderly; once or twice with some malice) that I can be beaten into the ground by willful, experienced guys who don't have half of my speed, a third of my brights, a fourth of my conditioning, a fifth of my talent. Not to mention what happens when I finally climb through the ropes with an obvious superior.

* * *

Stepping into the dank, musty gym, the Champ winks at spectators and approaches the ring with a big, easy smile, taking measured, self-contained steps on the balls of the feet, shoulders slightly back, chest out, head level. There's a regality to it. It is watchful, a little removed; cool but not snooty. As if the skin is listening. As if every pore contains a satellite dish. Boxers call this the champions' walk. Ali moves this way. So did "Sugar" Ray Robinson.

Using yellow elastic bandaging, the Champ quickly and expertly wraps wrists and hands, and ritualistically tugs on a pair of shining, fire-engine-red, twelve-ounce gloves. After wrapping ankles and feet, the Champ steps barefoot through the ropes to meet a strutting sparring partner. The sparring partner outweighs the titleholder by a good twenty pounds.

The bell rings and the Champ dances a few steps to the left, measuring the opponent with a couple jabs that miss.

Now inside, the Champ digs a straight right in under the sparring partner's rib cage, springs a hook in near the right kidney, crisply doubles it to the head, then dances to the side and out of reach, her blondish hair bounding behind her, cascading down her shoulders and spilling across her back in ringlets. She's wearing matching black shorts and a loose-fitting tank top.

She bends to the right and snaps a jab into my nose. My ears are already ringing from the good hook she caught me with. Now I blink back tears and stare at her. She's startlingly good-looking—high cheekbones and clear, bright, expansive eyes the hue of Western skies. Deltoids are large, firm, round; forearm muscle groups dance. Her musculature is so defined that fat cells seem to have no place to hide in her body. There's an aura of healthy tomboy androgyny around her: she's Doris Day with Bruce Lee–level musculature. All of this, of her, is more than a bit disarming.

Five-time women's featherweight world kickboxing champ Kathy Long drops her gloves to her sides, sticks her neck and face forward, teasing me. She pulls her head back and away when I try to pump a quick jab into her chin, and immediately leans back in, rapping my nose with a shocking straight left. It's a slick Ali-style trick I can't believe I've fallen for. My eyes haven't quit watering from the last shot she caught me with; there's no way I'll stop them now. My mouth feels fat and swollen, as if I'm sitting in a dentist's chair getting all my molars drilled into at once; it tastes like I've been trying to suck out the insides of someone's hundred-year-old bathroom plumbing.

Long slings a Thai-style switch-kick toward my head, which I slip. Before she gets her foot back to the floor, I manage to stick her (finally!) with a long, firm left; she makes me pay by kicking me hard on the inside of my left thigh. The slapping sound is explosive in the small room. I feel the pain after I hear the sound: a thousand fire ants sink scalpel-sharp nippers into some of the most tender flesh on my body.

No matter what, though, I'm not going to show Kathy she's gotten to me. I dance to the left, trying to seem relaxed and casual. She comes on, her lips squeezed together tightly, looking tombstone serious. I move to the ropes, then lean my upper body to the left, as if I'll disengage. She goes for my draw; I thump her with a straight right lead that snaps her head back sixty degrees. She's stunned—maybe. I move in fast and hard with both hands, shooting the best stuff I've got.

She covers up. The hooks and uppercuts I zip toward her head catch nothing but gloves and sweat. I step back and spring a left side-kick toward her belly. She grits her teeth, deflects the kick outwardly with her left elbow, turning me toward her, opening me up. I know what's coming, but there's no way to react quickly enough to do anything about it. She roars from her shell, drilling me hard and deep to my right shin with her own shin. The noise I hear is unmistakably that of bone against bone. The sound makes me wince. To put some space between Kathy and me, I slide off to the right. I'm okay, my leg is fine, just a little numb, I don't feel a thing. Then, without another shot being thrown, my leg gives out and I unexpectedly find myself looking up at her from the canvas. A goddamned delayed reaction. I feel like a soiled shirt tossed to the floor.

That's when the real pain arrives, powerful enough to separate thoughts from words. Everything I look at throbs. The air around me goes red-tinged. My leg feels as if it had decided to remove itself from my body and run into a wrought-iron coffee table at fifty miles an hour.

Although I can't hear a thing because of the white noise going off in my skull, I know I'm groaning loud and making ugly faces and looking about as dumb as a person can look. I roll to my right, hugging my shin, rocking from side to side; a father, clutching his young son's right hand, squinches up his face and subconsciously bends to the right to rub his own shin. Embarrassed, I roll in the other direction and close my eyes.

Kathy comes over, kneels, and tugs me to my feet. She places an arm around my waist to support me. I hobble from the ring, eyes pointed toward the floor. I can't carry weight on my right leg. Kathy gets me to a corner and sits me on a stool. As Kathy walks away, a smirking trainer with curly red hair comes over and straps ice packs to both of my thighs and my calves. "You just got beat up by a skirt," she says, trying not to giggle in my face.

"Hey, that's my life story," I say, head bowed.

I limp across the room and take a seat beside Kathy as she autographs publicity photos for a clot of spectators—"Hugs and punches from Kathy Long, five-time world champ."

After everyone but Kathy and I have left, she reaches into a pocket of her shorts and produces a necklace with an attached small gold boxing glove. It's the symbol that amateur boxers wear who have won Golden Gloves tournaments. The difference is that Kathy's pendant has a one-fourth-carat diamond that's been set in the palm of the glove. She straps this talisman about her neck and smiles a smile that levels me even more than her fists and feet. She smiles again, waves for me to follow her, and she walks the champions' walk back out onto the street.

4

My face has sprouted a thick glowing beard that I know I can't grow. I'm playing a flute. Not with mouth or hands. The pipe is part of my body. The instrument plays itself.

Behind me, in a mirror, stands a woman. She's young and strong. Bushels of long, loose curls spill from her shoulders. Her scent rises bright in the air. It's the fragrance of waterfalls and wind and the skin of peaches. She's admiring the music and its instrument.

She reads from a small, worn leather book. She says: Is not the flute that soothes, the very one carved from wood with knives?

*   *   *

Early summer 1976: a year of the dragon. I've felt for more than two years that this is when *this* has to happen.

The morning train rumbles by, its whistle moaning as the sound drifts in my window from over off Stratford Road. I lie in bed a few minutes and gaze at leaves on sugar maples in the backyard, and ones on the water oaks, and on the river birches, and the willows and weeping cherries, and at all the fescue sprouting in all the yards.

I stand, pull on a pair of white gym shorts, and ease into a few slow stretches, first palming the floor, then touching nose and chin to knees. I hobble to the kitchen, pop a couple slices of wheat bread in the toaster, open the refrigerator, and siphon a giant gulp of skim milk straight from the carton, then walk out to the front yard and draw a few deep breaths of air.

I watch the mailman make his rounds, the business guys all sad and empty-eyed on their way to the nine-to-fives, turn and stare at my earthen path, which follows the creek as it lopes lazily behind Dad's house, smile, and think, "Man, I'm one lucky son of a gun."

About noon, I lace up an old pair of Adidas, open the back door, and sprint across the yard and down to the creek, sail up the bank on the other side and onto my path. Smelly ol' Dallas falls in beside me. "Hey, woofa," I say, and bend to greet him with a tug on his flopping jowls.

I kick my legs high, churning stones and last year's leaves beneath my feet, take air in through mouth and nose, and blow it out in short, hot *fuuh*s. As we start up the short incline that leads to Shaffner, Dallas thunders ahead, his feet splashing waves of dust behind him. As I top the hill, I see him chasing two setters, one Irish, one English, through the field below.

At a dead run, I pump out the last two hundred yards between the dogs and me. As I run, I whip Dallas's leash from where I've been keeping it tied round my waist, and as I pull up beside him, I slap it on his collar. He realizes I've chained him, digs his claws into the turf, and heaves forward with his shoulders, dragging me a few feet before I yank him up short beside me.

"Davis, hey, where'd you get that big, weird mutt?" a girl's voice calls from between laughs behind me. I turn to find Emily Crews, a cute sixteen-year-old who's a customer at the convenience store—she regularly comes in to flirt and to buy sodas—standing a few feet away.

I explain that Dallas is no mutt, he's a full-blooded bullmatian, but she keeps on laughing. "Lyn," she calls over her shoulder, "you've got to see this dog. Davis says he's some kind of 'damnation.' Doesn't he look like Petie on *The Little Rascals*?"

A girl appears from behind a slab of limestone down by the creek. She's barefoot and wearing a pair of cutoffs and a skimpy white tank top. And she's bra-less. She has big brown animal eyes and almost waist-length curly auburn hair that's as thick as a horse's mane. I've seen this girl before. We talked a little at the party after my third kickboxing match.

She steps over and Emily introduces us. "Davis Miller, this is my friend Lyn Spencer."

Lyn smiles. My legs go weak and numb and my mouth feels that it may not work when I try to open it. "Davis," she says in a way I've never heard my name pronounced. "Davis Miller," she repeats, as if the words mean something. "You have a nice tan," she says.

I don't tell her that I don't have time to lie in the sun. "Thanks," I say, struggling to get out the words. "So do you."

* * *

On our first date, Lyn and I take in a movie. We go to see— what else?—*Enter the Dragon*, which has been rereleased and is playing downtown at the Carolina Theatre. The 1976 National AAU Boxing Championships are taking place in Winston-Salem this same weekend. During the movie, Ray Leonard,

Howard Davis, Michael and Leon Spinks, and other pugilists sit in the row behind us.

At the end, several boxers ask for a ride to their hotel. Lyn and I squeeze room for five of them in the Camaro, four in back, one up front. Lyn has to slide right up next to me (like I mind), one leg on each bucket seat and the gear shift between her thighs. We drive across town to the Ramada Inn near the airport. On the way we all talk about Lee. "Little man hits hard," one boxer says. "Looks like he hits hard as a heavyweight."

As we drop off the fighters, Lyn asks if I'll buy her a beer. We stop by the store and pick up a couple eight-ounce bottles of Miller, then drive to Shaffner Park. Almost as soon as I slip the gear shift up into park and switch off the lights, I feel compelled to show Lyn some of my very best stuff.

I get out of the car, kick off my sandals in the grass, do side stretches by placing one foot, then the other, atop the roof, then dance around the Camaro, zinging punches and kicks as quick and juicy as I ever have in my life, so fired up to be with her and finally have somebody to share *Enter the Dragon* with—not to mention loosened up by the first beer I've drunk in three years—that I do something I've never even thought about trying in front of anyone: I emulate Lee's tomcat-eating-a-chicken *kiai*.

"*Waa-saa!*" I screech, and look at Lyn for a reaction. She doesn't laugh at me. Her eyes are open saucer-wide and she's smiling. I think she's impressed.

*   *   *

101

At first: it's organs and blood, muscle and bones and connective tissue. There's the groping.

Then: "Trust me," you say. And you touch my hips, guiding me, yet allowing me to guide myself. Then that part of me that enters you becomes me, in that moment. Then there's not even that. No me, no you. Nothing to prove, nowhere to be, nothing larger to do.

5

"I am all styles yet I am no style," said Bruce Lee.

How and why did I come from martial art to make a life struggling to sculpt elegant sentences and paragraphs? Three (more) reasons worth mentioning: throw five thousand exacting punches and kicks per day for several years, and the idea of a rewrite or two isn't terribly imposing; after you've been hit in the face with a few qualified fists and feet, a couple humbling reviews ain't the most frightening of possibilities; and internalizing the intensity I found radiating from Lee allowed me to access the rigorous, beautiful, primeval writing place inside me.

Yet the very thing that gave me courage to write is that through my experiences in martial arts I'd learned not to take what I did, or didn't do, personally. I wasn't performing martial art, but was a vessel through which the art poured. And I would be a vehicle through which words flowed.

Oh, and one more thing. When I stumbled across Lee in *Enter the Dragon*, for the first time in my life, suddenly I was awake. Today, I still see with fresh eyes. I don't know of a quality more important (or more grandly discomforting) for someone who feels he needs to write.

*   *   *

All through the mid-1970s, until I met Lyn, Lee and his movies had been both my fever and the cure, the dream and the life. During that time, between rocketing tens of millions of kicks and hand-strikes, I'd studied *Enter the Dragon* and Lee's three other films dozens of times, regarding each of them as my own personal martial Rosetta Stone. Again and again, off I'd go, to my haven of fairy-tale violence, to the fabled land of Fistiana, that place where the plastic scars always stick and pigs' blood ceaselessly flows.

In 1973 and 1974, Lee's movies had been shown in middle-class shopping malls and uptown cinemas, but by 1975, in search of enlightenment, I'd descend into dark, cool confines of inner-city movie houses, the air reeking of urine and Thunder-bird wine. I'd take my seat among a couple dozen screaming black folks, a few aspiring white street toughs, and occasionally a drunk old man who'd wake from his catatonia, jump from his seat, and scream, "Kill that muhfucka," whenever charac-ters stopped talking and Lee hit someone.

All these years later, I reveal so much of my story not in self-revelation, and mostly not for ego gratification (after all, lots of it is as embarrassing as walking down a city street sporting dirty underwear atop my head), but because I believe it says much about Lee's screen image, the dream he developed, and the innate, supremely powerful effect he had—and continues to have—on his core audience: the lonely, the frustrated, the inar-ticulate, the disaffected, the downtrodden, the half-asleep.

*   *   *

Rarefied martial training—and through it the development of my writing skills—eventually took me many places. While studying creative writing at East Carolina University in Greenville, North Carolina, my first story for a national magazine, *Sports Illustrated,* was about a seminal experience with Muhammad Ali, a 1975 sparring session with him at his Pennsylvania training camp, when I was still hoping to become a great fighter myself. In September 1977, Lyn and I eloped and tried, unsuccessfully, to get married at the Ali–Earnie Shavers bout in Madison Square Garden. By 1986, when I became the district manager of a video store chain in Ali's hometown of Louisville, Kentucky (in 1982, desperately needing money, I'd chosen to work in a video store—my first full-time job—partly to watch Ali fights and Bruce Lee movies for free), I seldom thought about him. My day-to-day concerns revolved around Lyn, our two children, and my weekly paychecks.

My first day in Louisville, driving to one of my stores with the company president, he pointed across the street and said, "Muhammad Ali's mom lives there." From then on, whenever I passed by, my concentration was riveted on the house. On the Friday before Easter, 1989, a block-long white Winnebago was parked out front. The license plate read, THE GREATEST.

Plucking myself up, I went to the door of the Winnebago, knocked. Ali opened the door, looking as big as God. He leaned under the door frame to see me, waved me in, did magic tricks, invited me to stay for dinner. "You're sincere, I can tell," he said. "I can feel it rumblin' up from inside people." That evening would become, without question, one of the most resonant of my life.

For several years after that, I saw a lot of Ali. I wrote a couple of stories about him and our relationship, including one about that first meeting that won several national awards, has been anthologized numerous times, and began my career. Then came my first book, *The Tao of Muhammad Ali,* the story of the intersection of his life with mine. Because of Ali, I've found my voice: I am now a writer.

Growing up in the sixties and seventies, I thought of myself as following in the "way" (the Tao) of Ali. As an adult, I've come to regard Ali as sort of a subconscious Taoist; there is no way to define accurately who he is, no way to categorize him. There is something liberative about this, but not so emancipating as the time I've spent with him. Being around Ali has always emptied me, opened me up, freed me. He allows me to feel genuinely childlike, almost entirely unboxed, abidingly innocent.

In 1992, because of the success of my Ali stories, I was working as the boxing writer for *Sport* magazine. In addition to writing monthly features and regularly traveling to boxing events for *Sport* (where I continued to hang out with Ali), I worked out several times a week on a heavy bag and a speed bag and helped train amateur and professional kickboxers in southern California. That summer I wrote articles for *Sport,* for *Sports Illustrated,* and for the *Los Angeles Times* about Bakersfield resident and world-champion kickboxer Kathy Long.

Fred Weintraub, who had produced *Enter the Dragon,* read two of those pieces and asked me to script a ninety-minute-long documentary about Lee for Warner Brothers. Weintraub said that his feature would be released on videocassette, then cable TV, around the twentieth anniversary of Lee's death and the theatrical premiere of the big-screen film bio, *Dragon: The Bruce Lee Story.*

I accepted Weintraub's offer, excited that I'd finally get to write about Lee (something I had striven to do for nearly twenty years; even when writing about boxing and boxers, I'd sneak Lee allusions into every piece I could)—and doing so for the guy who had co-produced Lee's only American film. More important, I was subconsciously expecting that, as my adult relationship with Ali had gotten richer, rounder, and more full than that which I'd experienced as a kid, the same would be true of Lee now that he had once again come into my life.

I went into Weintraub's project knowing many of the surface details of Lee's story. Over the following months, working to puzzle out, to divine, some kind of greater truth about Lee, traveling to New York, Los Angeles, San Francisco, Seattle, and Hong Kong, spending time with and talking to his students, friends, co-workers, and some of his family, as was true of the time I've spent with Ali, I believe I found some things about Lee that might be called abiding.

But let me warn you before you read further: mostly, they are not what I could have expected or could ever have hoped for.

Section Three

A LITTLE HISTORY

Everything dies
Baby that's a fact
Maybe everything that dies
Someday comes back.

—BRUCE SPRINGSTEEN

Nineteen

FAME AS FACELESS AS GOD: few people have attained this, the ultimate, ethicless, unqualified fame. Among names that come to mind: Jesus, Buddha, Mohammed.

Perhaps only four people from the twentieth century can be considered for this list:

1—Adolph Hitler
2—Muhammad Ali (always Ali)
3—Elvis Presley
      and, yes, surprisingly,
4—Bruce Lee.

Vague visions of midnight street wars, lost powers, hidden rhythms, secret techniques—Vibrating Butterfly Palms, Delayed Death Touches, Sleeping Hands, Whirling Dragon Tails—swirl like exploding Chinese skyrockets seen through a mist.

Academy Award–winning actor James Coburn has said, "Bruce was more dynamic than anyone else I've met. He could go from zero to one-forty in no time at all—*pow!* and he'd be gone."

Movie director Blake Edwards has conjectured that the problem in his relationship with Lee "was that there was never a moment I wasn't in awe of him."

Academy Award–winning screenwriter Stirling Silliphant confided, "All my life I've known only idiots. I define an idiot as a person who makes himself less than he could be by blaming his actions on something, or someone, outside himself. The only non-idiot I've known, the only person I've seen who exercised his abilities, whether physical or intellectual, to the highest possible degree, is Bruce Lee."

Yet those who don't practice martial art regard Lee's movies almost as respectfully as Three Stooges shorts—Larry bonks Moe on his noggin, Moe sticks his fingers in Larry's eyes, Larry stomps on Curly's foot. But there are others who take Bruce Lee very seriously. Three decades after his death, Lee is revered by martial-arts practitioners throughout the world. His likeness is sold in boutiques in Beverly Hills and in souks in Marrakesh; it hangs on apartment walls in Kiev and in Paris, and in mud huts in central African nations and in the Australian outback, as well as on the insides of gym lockers in Peoria and Liverpool; as of the year 2000, his image is the one that's still most common on the cover of martial-arts publications worldwide; his ambiguous reputation as the twentieth-century god of martial art is known in almost every city, town, and village on the planet.

At the turn of the millennium, though relatively few of us have seen Lee or one of his four movies, his name may be recognized in more places than that of anyone else of our time. American Tae Kwon Do legend Jhoon Rhee tells of a 1992 trip to Russia: "When I went shopping in Moscow, everywhere there were Bruce Lee posters and Muhammad Ali posters. I asked a lot of people, 'Who is most famous, Muhammad Ali or Bruce Lee?' I was so surprised to hear, unanimously, 'Bruce Lee.'"

Within two years of Lee's death, his name had become a cliché. Bruce Lee: a pseudonym to be tagged onto every side-kicker in every dojo, arena, dojang, gym, *kwoon,* movie-studio lot, or back alley. Consider those Hong Kong movies of the mid-1970s that thoroughly diminished Lee's story and had titles such as *Bruce Lee Strikes Back from the Grave, The Clones of Bruce Lee,* and *Bruce Lee Goes to Hell,* and that starred a legion of grimacing and screeching, pseudo-similar androids such as Bruce Li, Bruce Le, Bruce Lei, Bruce Lo, Myron Bruce Lee, (Charles) Bronson Lee, Bruce LeRoy, Dragon Lee, Bruce Tease, Bruce Sleaze, Bruce Quease, Spruce Trees, Loose Leaves.

All these years later, a fog of rumor, myth, and mystery continues to surround the circumstances of Lee's death. Among the most popular stories are that he died from overtraining or from too much sex or was murdered by angry kung-fu masters; by the Chinese "Mafia"; by an evil herbalist; by a secret society of martial-arts assassins; by the director of his first two movies (fewer than three weeks before his death, Lee had threatened this director—who'd been goading him for months—with a knife hidden in his belt buckle); by the head of the movie studio for which he worked (who, through the remainder of the century, would reap hundreds of millions of dollars from Lee's legend); by rival Hong Kong movie magnates who were rumored to be jealous of, and infuriated by, Lee's success; by his lover(s); by his wife; by big mythological dragons angered that he had called himself Small Dragon Lee. Or that he had an unsuspected congenital condition that became lethal because of the intensity with which he lived. Maybe most fabulously, that Lee had not died, but had gone into seclusion, in the Shaolin temple/in a cave in the jungles of southeast Asia/on a remote mountaintop, and that he'd return at some date—perhaps the turn of the millennium. After all, 2000 is a year of the dragon. And Lee's sixtieth birthday.

To me, man-nova Bruce Lee's *real* life is more intriguing than these quasi-religious myths. Lee was a flawed, complex, yet singular talent whose reputation, in death, has been even more abused than Elvis's—Presley basics have been correctly reported hundreds of times. Yet, despite Lee's worldwide fame and his considerable effect on global culture, no one has written about him truthfully or well. Indeed, if Ali is the most famous fellow of the twentieth century whom we know most about, Lee is the one about whom we know least. Celluloid and print fictions have dramatically marginalized his reputation and his impact on society. Few of us have a clue what Lee said, felt, dreamed, and did or didn't do. The mist of money-making myth around him is so thick that the truth of his story has been almost entirely obscured. It's time some of this fog got burned away.

The reality is this: In the three years immediately preceding his death, Bruce Lee revolutionized the martial arts and forever changed action moviemaking. He became the first truly international film luminary (popular not only in the United States, Great Britain, and Europe, but in Asia, the Soviet Union, the Middle East, and on the Indian subcontinent; in those pre-Spielberg days, people in most nations were not necessarily worshipful of the Hollywood hegemony). Until now, Lee has received little credit for these accomplishments.

Think of Gatsby and his optimistic, orderly, yet doomed pursuit of the dream. An important literary figure begins to emerge, in the way that Ali and Elvis are characters of consequence—something in the beauty and the bones of these lives elevates biography into apologue.

Twenty

Kilimanjaro, at 19,710 feet,... *is said to be the highest
mountain in Africa. Its western summit is called the
Masai "Ngàje Ngài," the House of God. Close to the
western summit there is the dried and frozen carcass of
a leopard. No one has explained what the leopard
was seeking at that altitude.*

—ERNEST HEMINGWAY,
The Snows of Kilimanjaro

From 1974 through to the end of that decade, nearly all
martial arts magazines in the United States contained ads
for colored T-shirts emblazoned with a cartoon illustration of
Lee's image and the wishful proclamation BRUCE LEE LIVES.

We have the impression, when watching his movies, that he
arrived fully actualized; he had always been Bruce Lee, the god
of martial art. But even Hemingway's leopard must have worked
to reach the altitude at which he fell, beautiful and damned.

Lee was born in San Francisco in 1940. His parents named
him Li Jun Fan and, as was common, a Caucasian nurse arbi-
trarily entered the Christian name Bruce Lee on his birth certifi-

cate. His mother, Grace, the youngest daughter of an influential Shanghai entrepreneur, was half German; his father, Li Hoi Chuen, a popular and wealthy Hong Kong comic performer and movie actor (in the Hollywood hagiography, *Dragon: The Bruce Lee Story*, Lee's father is anonymous, widowed, and nearly impoverished), was touring the U.S.A. as a major performer with a Peking opera troupe.

Bruce Lee's had been a show-business family for many generations. The elder Lee arranged his son's first part in a movie: Bruce Lee appeared in a Hong Kong picture when he was three weeks old; he was six when his father helped him get his first starring role.

Lee grew up in his parents' home on the Kowloon side of Hong Kong, not, as was claimed in *Dragon*, as an only child, but with two brothers (one older, one younger), two sisters (one older, one younger), a pet monkey, and several servants. The adolescent Bruce Lee was frisky and mischievous; his family's Cantonese nickname for him translates as "Never Sits Still."

Throughout the 1970s, sitting in movie theaters dreaming about being his friend and private student on the set of *Enter the Dragon,* I regarded Lee the same way most fans still think of him: as the character in *Enter the Dragon*—a man alone, attuned to the natural world and his inner rhythms, a man clean of secondary wisdom. The historical Lee was different from my martial dreams: he admired and was influenced not so much by Shaolin monks as by Elvis, James Dean, and Jerry Lewis—whose facial expressions and body habits are observable in Lee's childhood movies as well as in the films he made as an adult—and by Hong Kong movies about kung-fu masters. By his eighteenth year, Lee was a major teen idol in Hong Kong who had starred in twenty films (none about martial arts), the most popular of which was *The Orphan,* in which he played a troubled adolescent in the James Dean style.

At thirteen he began to study wing chun *gung-fu* (the Cantonese pronunciation of *kung-fu,* which Lee himself used). Movie lore has it that he was a starship-quick and religiously obsessive student. In actuality, he was most interested in acting, in girls, though he was basically shy with them, and in dancing—he became the cha-cha champion of Hong Kong—and didn't take serious interest in wing chun until years later.

It has always been written that Lee studied gung-fu directly under Yip Man, the aged, esteemed head of the wing chun clan. As evidence, we have the famous photo of the venerated old opium smoker standing to the left of his fifteen-year-old pupil, smiling benevolently and looking as ancient, leathered, wise, fetal, and transcendent as a mummy. Yearbook picture notwithstanding, old Professor Yip supervised senior students and instructors; Bruce Lee was not one of these. Indeed, all indications are that Lee never had a single lesson with Master Yip. The future king of gung-fu's primary teacher was Wong Shum Leung, who describes the one fight in which he saw the teenage Lee participate:

"We had contests on rooftops with other gung-fu schools. These were common in Hong Kong and were not dangerous. One time we took Bruce along with the seniors. He did okay in the first round, but then he said that he didn't want to fight. 'I wanta go home,' he said.

"We told him if he didn't go back in there, we'd show him

what real fighting was—he'd have to fight us. He was scared, but he went back and finished his opponent fast."

Bruce Lee legend tells this quite another way. According to popular myth, in his late teens, the apprentice god of martial art regularly fought in organized, weekly, illegal rooftop contests not dissimilar to seedy backroom bare-knuckle boxing smokers. Lee soon became the baddest boy in the Crown Colony. In his final rooftop battle, his opponent's skull was fractured. Since Lee was a well-known delinquent, police knocked on the door of Li Hoi Chuen asking questions; the elder Lee saved face and Bruce Lee's life (a rival gang would surely kill his famous, street-hard son), by banishing him to the United States. These fables are indicative of much that devotees believe they "know" about Lee.

The reality of how he came to the United States more closely resembles this: his influential dad didn't think the boys that waggish young Bruce had begun hanging out with were good influences. It would best serve his impetuously curious son to move to the States and stay with upstanding family friends in San Francisco.

*   *   *

In most ways, Bruce Lee's adjustment to life in America was not unconventional for a Hong Kong Chinese immigrant. Within weeks of arriving, he left San Francisco for Seattle, where he struggled to improve his English and get a high school degree at Edison Technical Institute; he later attended the University of Washington as a philosophy major; he excelled in some classes, and managed to survive most others, partly by trading gung-fu lessons with better-rounded students who agreed to write papers for him. He found a wife at university (not the sexually aggressive, genius cheerleader in *Dragon,* but a timid and inexperienced, sweet and sleepy-looking coed named Linda Emery), he quit school and along the way made a decision that was not at all conventional: he was going to become the best martial artist in the history of the world. Best. Ever. Period. No contest. Amen.

At gung-fu demonstrations in Seattle, Lee attracted the same sorts of people who would later become his most obsessive movie fans. "Tough guys *and* wimps flocked to Bruce," says Jesse Glover, Lee's first-ever pupil.

Although *Dragon,* numerous Hong Kong movies, and many of his own students perpetrate the Lee myth that he was a brilliant and anxious martial-arts instructor, the historical Lee reluctantly began to teach mostly because he needed money and didn't want a job to get in the way of his own martial training. "He didn't have the patience to teach," explains Jim DeMile, another Seattle student. "Bruce was a self-serving guy. He didn't see a reason to teach. He used us to improve his own skills, which isn't the same as teaching."

Lee and his wife moved to Oakland, California, in 1963, looking for a better market to make money from gung-fu. On the first of February, 1965, the last day of that year of the dragon, a son, Brandon, was born. Lee opened a gung-fu school near San Francisco's Chinatown. In the 1960s, gung-fu was basically unknown to westerners. Many Chinese practitioners taught only other Chinese (as much because Chinese were the only ones interested as because of their legendary ethnocentricity). People from numerous ethnic backgrounds came to Lee; he taught anyone he wanted. He and his pupils wore street clothes when they practiced, and he had no ranking system— his students wore no black and colored belts. What's more, Lee was not shy about his belief that, to teach, he didn't need the support or approval of elders in the San Francisco Chinese community.

Concerned that they had lost face, those elders sent a representative to confront him. "This guy came into Bruce's school," explains Dan Inosanto, a longtime Lee pupil. "He said, 'If you beat me, you can teach. If I beat you, you got to close your school.'"

In *Dragon,* this encounter is re-created as a high-kicking duel to the death between two screaming, posing, gymnastic athletes who are as hard-bodied, fierce, and lethal as human-sized yellow jackets. Lee is paralyzed by his evil, dirty-fighting opponent (who uses precisely the sort of tactics the historical Lee would have), and becomes depressed until he is coaxed out of his funk by the always beautiful and eternally optimistic Linda, who reinvigorates his shattered will and inspires him to write a brilliant philosophical treatise, titled *The Tao of Jeet Kune Do,* about his transcendent martial art. This manuscript is published, almost overnight, as a respected mainstream book; its success and his wife's constant ministrations motivate Lee miraculously to cure his own paralysis.

This Hollywood revision trivializes not only Lee's life—as well as our concepts of love, work, art, and serious illness—but his effect on the martial arts. My experiences as a sixteen- and seventeen-year-old in a western North Carolina karate class were far from unique. Before Lee, the vast majority of martial practitioners all over the world were basically incapable of defending themselves; athletes as we think of them in the West simply didn't exist in the Asian fighting disciplines.

"When we fought in tournaments and in schools," says first world heavyweight kickboxing champion and former Lee student Joe Lewis, "we tried to imitate real fighting by throwing what were supposed to be killing blows. We'd fire one kick or punch and wouldn't hit nothing, then stop and wait for the ref to call a point. There was no tactical movement, no defense to speak of, and no credit for how tough you were or weren't— because nobody was getting hit. More than anything, it was a game of tag. How can you call that fighting?"

Fellow kickboxing pioneer Don "The Dragon" Wilson says of his first ring fight, which took place in 1974, "I was so scared I was shaking. I honestly thought that when I hit somebody or he hit me, the one who got caught first would be killed on the spot. That's pretty much what everybody thought back in those days, before we knew that's not the way it works. Nobody had ever really tried all this 'lethal' karate-shit before we did."

In the real-world version of Lee's Oakland scrap, his puny, timid, underqualified opponent turned and ran as Lee chased him around a room. With closed fists (because he didn't know better), Lee pounded the back of his challenger's head. Lee's hands became painfully swollen and, gasping for breath, he tackled his opponent, pinned down his arms, and sat on him.

Although Lee had "won" this encounter, it woke him up (*What if this guy had been a* real *mean-ass?* Lee must have wondered), and brought on a period of considerable introspection.

With what was as much shaky-ego bolstering and an obsession for success as a passion for knowledge (isn't this true for most twenty-five-year-olds?), he began a process of reading, ruminating, and training—of what has since been described as moment-by-moment reinvention.

Over the next few years Lee became the first Western-style athlete in the martial disciplines. He ran, pushed weights, jumped rope, performed staggering numbers of calisthenics, punched numerous kinds of bags, developed dozens of pieces of training equipment that he used daily—many of which, after his death, were adopted by the burgeoning community of martial arts practitioners.

"No one ever trained as fanatically as Bruce," says Chuck Norris, who became one of Lee's pupils. "He seemed to train twenty-four hours a day."

This ongoing sojourn in the internal wilderness became the basis of the revolution that Lee would lead in the martial arts. (In the mid- to late 1970s, like lots of guys, I spent hundreds and hundreds of dollars on equipment that I believed Lee might have used or invented. I opened every corrugated paper box that arrived from martial-arts supply companies as if it protected the martial equivalent of the Dead Sea Scrolls.) Bruce "Never Sits Still" Lee had adopted the distinctly American faith: that we can invent ourselves on a daily basis. And that we can work to become whatever and whomever we want.

He gave a demonstration of his method, which he called Jun Fan gung-fu, named after himself, at a martial-arts tournament in Los Angeles. Film of that demo was shown to *Batman* television series producer William Dozier, who called Lee in for a screen test and eventually cast him as Kato in the *Green Hornet* TV series.

In the spring of 1966, the Lee family moved to Los Angeles, where a daughter, Shannon, was born and twenty-six episodes of *The Green Hornet* were filmed. The show ran on ABC for one season. It was the first time that Chinese martial art had been broadcast on national network American television. *The Green Hornet* brought Lee to the attention of American martial practitioners, most of whom had not heard of him. Pan American Games 1967 judo gold medalist Hayward Nishioka describes seeing Lee on television. "As soon as he came on, you knew he knew his stuff. For the first time ever on TV or in the movies, it wasn't hokey, it wasn't fake, it wasn't trick photography. It was real moves being executed with excellence."

Karate competitor Bob Wall, who would later co-star with Lee in two movies, reinforces Nishioka's reaction. "Because of Bruce, everybody I knew in the martial arts were fans of *The Green Hornet*. Nobody, and I mean nobody, missed the show. We wished it was *The Bruce Lee Show* and he'd be fighting in every frame."

Respected veteran stuntman Gene LeBell, who regularly worked on *The Green Hornet* and had toiled for many years as a bouncer and as a pro wrestler, has his own, less enthralled, way of describing Lee and his role as Kato: "Bruce was a driver that drove the star around and wore a black outfit and a little hat."

I, too, saw Lee in 1966, though it would be late 1973 before I'd remember having done so. My father and Carol and I were visiting an aunt, uncle, and cousins in Charlotte. The Saturday morning after Thanksgiving, we drove from Uncle John's house on the outskirts of the city to the Christmas parade downtown. The sky was clear and bright. From Uncle John's third-floor office window, we stared down on the procession of clowns, cowboys on horseback, high school marching bands, and civic officials and beauty queens wearing thick overcoats, who waved and smiled and blew vapor into the air from convertibles. Twenty minutes into the show, an innocuous white float passed our building. Several people were standing on the float, waving to kids and parents who lined the streets. The smallest person on the float was standing at the very front, by himself. He was wearing a black suit and mask, shiny gloves, and a billed hat; he was waving his right arm and, like everyone else, his breath disappeared in the air.

"Who's that?" I asked my cousin Brent.

"That's Kato," he replied. "On TV."

I didn't give the guy on the float another thought. Nothing about Bruce Lee felt important or even interesting on that cold Saturday morning in November 1966.

*   *   *

Lee himself was not keen on his co-starring role in *The Green Hornet*. He wanted to make "real" movies, be a "real" actor. Although he was frustrated by the robotics of playing Kato (before and since Lee, martial-arts characters on TV and in the movies have always been less than human and little more than fighting robots, even when cast in lead parts) and his subsequent lack of acting jobs, he didn't despair. Linda took a job as a secretary, which allowed her husband the opportunity to commit himself yet more rigorously to his aspiration of becoming the world's most complete fighter.

"She gave him what he wanted," explains James Coburn, who was a friend, benefactor, and one of Lee's Los Angeles pupils. "She left him alone, gave him comfort when he needed it, had children, and did everything for them. It kept him free. There was a kind of Asian subservience to it."

Where most martial practitioners in the world slavishly followed one style of combat or another, Lee analyzed and experimented with dozens of combat systems, including numerous styles of gung-fu and karate, as well as Tae Kwon Do, judo, and jujitsu, and Western boxing, wrestling, fencing (which Lee became interested in because his older brother, Peter, was accomplished with a foil), and the French foot-fighting sport called *savate*. His stated goal was to distill the essence—that which was most efficient and practical—from each martial system.

Chief among Lee's influences was Muhammad Ali. Lee, whose primary fighting stance was right-side forward, where Ali faced left, bought film of every Ali bout that he could find. Watching Ali's image in mirrors so that he could more easily understand what Ali was doing, Lee attempted to emulate Ali's movements. In *Enter the Dragon,* as Lee danced around a shocked-from-his-socks, then knocked-on-his-twat Bob Wall, he was trying to replicate both Ali's footwork and facial expressions. And, like Ali, the Bruce Lee in *Enter the Dragon* always wore white or black or a combination of the two. (This style, this perceived relationship with Ali—and therefore with me—was not a small part of what first pulled me to Lee.) "Bruce idolized Ali, his brilliance, his footwork, his speed, his fluidity, his elusiveness," says Joe Lewis. "He felt that Ali was the best there was."

Chunks of Lee's movie fight with Chuck Norris in *Way of the Dragon*, in which he makes Norris look like so much gray cube-steak being broiled on a jet-air grill—Lee bounds about a stationary Norris, coming down from his toes to blister the latter with a phantasm of too-quick-to-count punches—are lifted almost exactly from moments in the second and third rounds of Ali's *real* bout with Cleveland Williams and the third-round knockout in the Brian London fight. Or, more precisely, from television camera angles of the Ali-Williams and Ali-London contests.

Says Lewis: "Bruce'd play the Williams fight over and over on that little eight-millimeter movie projector he had. First round, Ali's purposely *just* out of range; Round Two, he catches Williams mid-range; Round Three, Ali kisses him good night. Bruce went over this again and again. We'd study the way Ali punched, the way he moved, his ability to control an opponent even while backing up. Bruce emphasized mobility. Karate people were using stationary stances. One of the keys to defensive superiority is not to give your opponent a stationary target. Ali did that better than anyone. He was Bruce's hero until the day Bruce died."

UCLA and Los Angeles Lakers basketball legend Kareem Abdul Jabbar, another of Lee's Hollywood students, says, "Bruce was in awe of Ali. He said he wanted to train Ali how to kick. Bruce said if he could do that, Ali'd be on another planet."

Wing chun had few kicking techniques; the kicks that Lee would have used in combat would have been thrown (sensibly) to the ankles, knees, groin, and coccyx. Throughout the 1960s, Lee developed not only his street-fighting skills but a spectacular, high-kicking, movie martial art (though he never became a particularly good high kicker). Coburn explains further: "Bruce sucked up everything he could apply to his art. If it worked, it worked. If it didn't, out it went. All philosophers, all training, all teaching, everything. If it works, you do it. And you only find out if it works *by* doing it. The rest of it's all jive."

Lee called his street-fighting method *jeet kune do,* which translates most accurately as "stop fist way," though it usually has been translated, less meaningfully, as "way of the intercepting fist." Lee's movie martial art is often incorrectly referred to as jeet kune do.

"There are three opportunities to strike an opponent," he said. "Before he attacks, during his attack, or after he attacks." In the jeet kune do of the mid-1960s, Lee attempted to focus on pre-attack options, working from the naïve notion that the fighter who moves most economically and efficiently, in a properly anticipatory fashion, will beat his opponent to the punch. (Yeah, okay, but what happens after that, when the guy doesn't fall down?)

Eventually, Lee regretted having given his art a name. "I am all styles, yet I am no style," he said. He had labeled, and thereby limited, that which he thought of as limitless, formless, beyond definition.

"He says JKD has no technique," Dan Inosanto notes. "My wife says everybody in the sixties talked that way."

Like all of us, the "limitless, formless" Bruce Lee was an ambiguous character driven by his biology, his acculturation, his chronological age, and his time: the 1960s and 1970s, that era when self-invention—the notion that you can cut yourself loose from psychic and physical moorings and float free, beyond the pull of gravity—seemed most possible a time that spawned an entire worldwide generation of mystics, a phenomenon that surely had never before happened.

I slowly stand, step to the mirrors, and leap into a jumping, spinning crescent kick. When I should plop to the floor, I keep levitating up. I cross my legs, close my eyes, sit on the air and float.

On a trip to Bombay with Coburn and Stirling Silliphant, Lee visited a school that taught a traditional Indian martial art. The class had not heard of him. After Lee gave an impromptu demonstration dressed in street clothes, the amazed instructor and his pupils bowed to him on hands and knees. One can't feed two kids and a wife, though, by being placed on a pedestal as the god of gung-fu. And the unemployed actor found it necessary to return to the role of martial-arts instructor.

Lee had never particularly enjoyed teaching, but now he was bored with it. He wanted to showcase his mushrooming skills before a larger audience than he'd attract to a martial-arts class; he felt that he needed, and deserved, to be internationally famous. To Lee, the best way to accomplish this would be to educate the entire world to Eastern culture and his ideas of what martial art *should* be—while validating his own shining existence.

Young Bruce Lee knew one place to seize this shimmering

future. The place that he knew was the perfect, the obvious, the only vehicle that could transport his martial art to the world. Bruce Lee, child of the movies, whose ideals of a gung-fu master came from films he'd loved as a child, made the decision to pursue his singular art in this singular way: he'd become the world's best-known martial artist by becoming the first genuinely international movie star.

In 1969, inspired by a mail-order course from self-motivational speaker Napoleon Hill, Lee wrote a letter to himself: "I, Bruce Lee, will be the highest-paid...superstar in the United States. In return, I will give the most exciting performances and render the best of quality in the capacity of an actor. Starting in 1970, I will achieve world fame and from then onward till the end of 1980, I will have in my possession $10,000,000. I will live the way I please and achieve inner harmony and happiness."

Section Four

THE SECRET DEATH OF AN

AMERICAN DRAGON

He grows enormously
and begins to live   *outside*
of time
outside *of space*
outside

of language *because*

he's no longer here.

—FROM A CONVERSATION WITH LEE FAMILY FRIEND SHELTON CHOW, WHO PARAPHRASES A. E. HOUSMAN'S "TO AN ATHLETE DYING YOUNG"

Twenty-one

FROM THE LATE 1970s through the early 1990s, Brooklyn resident and documentary film producer George Tan traveled again and again from New York to Los Angeles to Seattle to San Francisco to Hong Kong. The purpose of Tan's quest: "There was almost no valid information about the guy. I was looking for the real Bruce Lee, not some gung-fu wizard. I followed the yellow brick road. Finally, I reached Oz and found the man behind the curtain."

One of Tan's basic discoveries on his fifteen-year odyssey (during which he became the world's premier Bruce Lee authority), and what I found on my own sojourn, is this: "In the history of movies," says Tan, "there's never been anyone else like Bruce. If Clint Eastwood had been a sheriff who became Christian about the whole thing and decided to show real sheriffing and had chosen movies as the medium, you could compare that to Bruce Lee."

From 1967 to 1971, Lee taught many notables in the film community, including, among others, actors James Coburn, Steve McQueen, Lee Marvin, Elke Sommer, and Sharon Tate; directors Blake Edwards and Roman Polanski; screenwriters Stirling Silliphant and Joe Hyams; and Warner Brothers president Ted Ashley. For those connected to the industry, those shepherds of the shimmering dream, Bruce Lee became the ideal of the martial monk, the wise man of gung-fu. (It was also during this time that Linda Lee came to adopt a particularly reverential stance toward her husband, sitting beside him, silently mouthing his words as he spoke.)

"Now, when I look at photos of Bruce and Linda together," says Tan, "him and those huge-ass forearms, her all long-limbed and gawky and repressed, what I see is not Master and Ms. Martial Monk but Popeye and Olive Oyl. Bruce's philosophizing came when he needed to develop an image, a device to market his martial art. He realized that there was more to be made from philosophizing than from getting punched in the face."

As Lee had incorporated elements from gung-fu, boxing, judo, karate, and so forth, to create his fighting methods, he looked to the writings of popular 1960s sages to develop "his" philosophy. In addition to Napoleon Hill, he was taken with Zen rebel Alan Watts and anti-mystic Jidu Krishnamurti, who, at the age of ten in southern India, had been adopted by elders from the Theosophical Society, a mystical order who took him to be a reincarnated embodiment of the Hindu god Krishna.

At thirty-four, after being extensively schooled in Britain, Krishnamurti renounced (and disbanded) the Theosophists, but not his role as "World Messenger," and spent the remainder of his ninety-one years delivering the message that, by their very separatist natures, religions and organized philosophies are obstacles to truth. Aphorisms attributed to Lee, which are now echolalically quoted by his widow, students, and followers, were lifted directly from Krishnamurti's work.

"Truth is not something dictated by your pleasure or pain," wrote Krishnamurti, "or by your conditioning as a Hindu or whatever religion you belong to. The man who is really serious, with the urge to find out what truth is, what love is, has no concept at all. He lives only in what is."

The Tao of Jeet Kune Do is not, as was claimed in *Dragon,* the masterwork greatly influenced by Linda Lee as a twenty-three-year-old Bruce Lee lay paralyzed in a hospital. It's simply an ongoing collection of notes that Lee did not intend to publish, but which were, posthumously, by his still-enthralled widow. In these notes Lee wrote, "Fighting is not something dictated by your conditioning as a kung-fu man, a karate man, a judo man, or whatnot. The man who is really serious, with the urge to find out what truth is, has no (martial arts) style at all. He lives only in what is."

Lee also created his wisdom from Chinese clichés (the "pointing finger" analogy is an example) and adapted at least one of Mao Tse-tung's credos. "Absorb what is useful; reject what is useless," Mao said. Lee expanded this to include, "Add specifically what is your own."

To say that a young person was not a great thinker, that he claimed others' thoughts as his own partly as a marketing ploy, is of course neither uncommon nor a crime. Nor do I mean to suggest that Lee didn't take these "non-ideas" seriously. After all, he'd been interested in philosophy as an adolescent, had majored in it at university, and had later collected such books by the hundreds, as well as any and all new and old volumes that he could find about martial arts, boxing, wrestling, and filmmaking. Lee's martial library consisted of thousands of books, many of which were long out of print and rare, and which he annotated and cross-annotated with personal training notes.

"I saw Bruce as a renegade Taoist priest," says a chuckling Kareem Abdul Jabbar. "He was into spirituality and it was heavily influenced by Taoism. But you couldn't put him in that box, he was beyond all that."

George Tan has a different take on Lee: "Bruce liked to use the word 'Tao'; he used it over and over. And the commonly held view is that Bruce was *sort of* Taoist. The truth, in a lot of ways, is that he was more Confucian. Taoists surf the waves; the basic idea of Taoism is to accept the world as it is. Taoists don't blow their horns in traffic. Confucians manipulate the world; they think it's here to serve them, not much different from the way Christians believe they reign over everything else. Bruce is a guy who believed he had somewhere to go—and he believed he *had* to get there quick. He wasn't about to let anybody get in his way. Bruce was a Confucian in Taoist clothing."

To support his role as the nonmaster master, Bruce Lee, the "I'm above competition" Taoist marketing guru, went out of his way to recruit the three most successful American sport karate competitors of the 1960s as *his* students. He offered free private instruction to Joe Lewis, Chuck Norris, and Mike Stone.

Lewis gives Lee considerable credit for his success as a sport fighter. "When I began working with Bruce, I became a much better competitor. I won ten consecutive grand championships without a loss. That was unheard of then and, hell, it's unheard of today. And what Bruce showed me enabled me to do that."

"Fighting, as is, is simple and total," Lee wrote. "The core of understanding lies in the individual mind, and until that is touched, everything is uncertain and superficial. After all, knowledge in the martial arts ultimately means self-knowledge."

In the years since Lee's death, the notion that we can be whatever we want, that we can liberate ourselves, has become the stuff of corporate advertising, of the self-help genre of nonwriting, of government-sanctioned propaganda, of half-hour infomercials. In the late 1960s the concept of self-actualization seemed shining, innocent, alive, and new.

As the aggressively self-actualized Bruce Lee employed his relationships with Lewis, Stone, and Norris to establish, then support, his reputation as the world's premier professor of fighting disciplines, Bruce Lee the performer used movie-industry students to try to convince major Hollywood producers that martial-arts scenes would have more sizzle than the "ham-fisted" John Wayne–style film fights of the day. Although celebrity pupils, particularly Stirling Silliphant, helped him get parts on several TV shows and a few films, including, among others, *Longstreet, Ironsides,* and *Blondie,* and the James Garner movie *Marlowe,* no one took this little Chinese fellow seriously enough to give him a chance as a star.

"Never sits still." Never gives up. In 1970, Lee had a story idea called *The Warrior,* about a Shaolin priest's adventures in the American West, which he took to friends at Warner Brothers, including producer Fred Weintraub, who liked the idea and wrangled money to create a ninety-minute pilot for television.

Around this time, Lee transcribed a rhyme for his friend Jhoon Rhee, and mailed it to him in Washington, D.C.

Am I a giant among men,
Master of all I survey,
Or an ineffectual pygmy
who clumsily blocks his own way?

WHICH ARE YOU?

The doubters said,
"Man cannot fly,"
The doers said,
"Maybe, but we'll try,"
And finally soared
Into the morning glow,
While non-believers
Watched from below.

So damn the torpedo. full speed ahead! Remember
what this Chinaman say 'Circumstances? Hell! I
make circumstances!'

> *Peace and inner harmony,*
> *Bruce*

Lee told James Coburn that on a regular one-hour television series he could take the necessary time to educate viewers to his philosophy and his art. This was something he'd never be able to accomplish in movies, he said. Lee boasted to American martial-arts magazine editors that Warner Brothers had offered him the lead in his own series.

What he didn't know was this: "He came into my office swing-
ing his nunchuks and jumping up and down for what must've
been ten minutes," says a former Warner Brothers television executive. "We never seriously considered him for the role."

Lee's story idea eventually became the *Kung Fu* TV series,
which, in the dubious tradition of Fu Manchu, Charlie Chan,
and Mr. Moto, starred Caucasian non-martial artist David Carradine, who, week after week, shuffled across deserts and
through cow towns in varying states of consciousness. Tan says
of the series, "What was passed off as Taoism and Buddhism
were writers' childhood Torah teachings filtered through West
Coast big bucks and pseudo-hippie aesthetics."

Carradine's character on the show was Chinese gung-fu master Kwai Chang Caine, the role the world's most relentlessly
conditioned Chinese martial-arts practitioner had conceived—
and coveted—for himself, but for which he received no credit.

*   *   *

In April 1970, Lee returned to Hong Kong to visit his mother
and brother Robert (his father had died in 1965). For the first
time, *The Green Hornet* was playing in Hong Kong, and Lee
was surprised to find that he was *almost* a celebrity, a minor
hero. He had left Hong Kong a well-known problem child and
had returned transformed, enlightened, a master of a new form
of gung-fu (martial art is as revered by the Chinese as Christianity was by sixteenth-century Puritans), a local boy who had
"made good" on the fabled Gold Mountain of Hollywood.

Lee appeared with five-year-old son Brandon on the Hong
Kong television talk show *Enjoy Yourself Tonight,* where the

audience *ooh*ed and *aah*ed over an uncommonly charismatic and board-shattering demonstration of his martial art, and where Lee introduced his heretical fistic philosophy to knowledgeable Hong Kong viewers. Twelve-year-old David Lo, movie director Lo Wei's son, was watching the show. The younger Lo excitedly told his father about Lee's demonstration.

Lo Wei remembered Lee from *The Orphan* and from several other films. Lo called the head of Hong Kong's fledgling Golden Harvest studios, Raymond Chow, to tell him about Lee. Chow, a runaway executive from the powerful Shaw Brothers Studios, was regarded by his former benefactor, Run Run Shaw, as a renegade and an outlaw. Not a bad fit for gung-fu rebel Bruce Lee.

Shortly after Lee returned to Los Angeles from Hong Kong (at almost exactly the time that he realized he'd always be treated as a Third World citizen in Hollywood), Chow offered a two-picture deal for $7,500 per movie, which Lee would accept.

Says Tan, "With the release of his first movie, *The Big Boss* (retitled *Fists of Fury* for U.S. distribution in 1972), in which he was not originally intended to be the star, Bruce became as big a celebrity in Hong Kong as the Beatles had been in England."

The reason: "His vitality was extraordinary," says Fred Weintraub. "No one had ever seen anything like Bruce. The life-force was just staggering."

Twenty-two

IN 1971, *THE BIG BOSS* and Lee's second movie, *Fist of Fury* (later renamed *The Chinese Connection* in the United States), kicked the stuffings out of box-office records throughout southeast Asia. In Singapore, showings were postponed because of traffic jams caused by fans. Throughout the Orient, both movies played continually for nearly ten years.

"We are not the sick men of Asia," Lee's screen character proclaimed to Japanese persecutors in *Fist of Fury/The Chinese Connection*. With this single declaration (scripted by Lo Wei), several thousand punches and kicks, and an avenging-tomcat-from-hell battle scream that the star created expressly for this picture, Bruce Lee transcended pop-idol status and came to be regarded as a messiah not only by millions of Hong Kong Chinese, but eventually by hundreds of millions of put-upon people throughout the world.

By the time Lee completed his third picture, the self-written, -directed, and -produced *Way of the Dragon,* he was developing the reputation, at least in Asia, that he'd been seeking, as the greatest fighter on the planet.

In early 1972, Lee brought his wife and children to Hong Kong from Los Angeles. After they'd settled in, he all but ignored them. Says Tan, "By then, he was getting all the adulation he could ever want. He had alternative sources of affection."

Where, in the States, Lee had effectively been a sexual neuter, Hong Kong women found him irresistible. They regarded him as worldly, mysterious, scholarly, sensitive, the equivalent of the male ideal in Western romance novels. He took at least one mistress; other lovers included co-stars. In Hollywood, Lee had worn kaftans, dashikis, and Nehru jackets. In Hong Kong he bought a floor-length mink coat, Elvis-style sunglasses, a red Mercedes convertible. Worldwide, he became a legend among martial-arts students. Larry Tan, who would later become a kung-fu teacher and choreograph martial-arts fights for several American movies, including *Remo Williams* and *The Wanderers,* describes an unexpected 1972 meeting with his childhood idol:

"There's never been anything in America like Bruce's fame in Hong Kong. He was on the cover of every single magazine—men's, women's, family magazines, it didn't matter. I saw him coming out of a restaurant. I'm at the bottom of these steps waiting for him to come down, waiting to meet my hero. I'm expecting a warrior-monk, this character out of his movies. What I got was Mr. Vegas.

"His cologne—it's so overpowering I smell him before I see him. The first thing I see is this pair of four-inch platform heels. He's wearing bell bottoms, this flowery shirt and jacket, huge sunglasses. I couldn't believe how tiny he was. Now, as an adult, I look back and see that he was this little, insecure guy who'd transformed himself on-screen into a physical giant."

In mid-1972 Lee starred in, wrote, co-produced, and directed the supposedly autobiographical *Way of the Dragon,* in which he played a bumpkin who's a gung-fu genius. In Hong Kong and Taiwan, *Way of the Dragon* quickly became known as Lee's religious affirmation of his own Chineseness. (In China the chief religion is not Taoism or Buddhism. Nor is it Confucianism or Maoism. The main religion among Chinese *is* Chinese, the religion of being Chinese, as being Jewish means more to those who are Hebrew than simple religion and ethnicity.) *Way of the Dragon* cemented Lee's Hong Kong reputation, and later his reputation worldwide, as a populist, a hero of common folk.

Lee choreographed all of the fights for *Way of the Dragon*, easily the most substantive and real-seeming of his movie battles, many of which are remarkable even after hundreds of viewings (the short fight with Bob Wall, just before his more famous contest with Chuck Norris, has a particularly powerful verisimilitude to it); he also dubbed English voices onto the Mandarin soundtrack, and played percussion for the score.

Privately he studied the complex rhythms of Hindu music, hoping to apply them to the flow of combat and of fight-scene choreography; he experimented with electric shock to speed his reaction time; had the sweat glands removed from under his arms because he didn't like the way his dripping pits looked onscreen; drove open fingers into closed steel cans of cola. He said that, before the end of 1973, he'd plunge his fingers *through* pine boards—a feat that surely had never been accomplished. After his death, boards would be found in his home with dramatic indentations in the wood.

He began receiving movie offers from around the world, and told friends that he'd become the martial-arts world's emissary for global harmony. Bruce Lee, the bringer of internationalism, the harbinger of one-world culturization that must take place in the twenty-first century.

Never sits still. Always reinventing. He wanted his next movie, *Game of Death,* to be a philosophical non-sermon about the necessity of being personally adaptable not only as a warrior, but as a person. He planned to open the movie with a shot of a cedar bough breaking under weight of snow, followed by one of a river reed bending in the wind.

In letters to friends, he wrote that he'd return to live in Hollywood and that he'd move his privately trained school of stuntmen, which included the likes of Jackie Chan and Samo Hung (who fought Lee in the opening contest in *Enter the Dragon*), with him. There were rumors that, after his return to the States, he would divorce Linda.

"He'd been drinking cow blood," says Coburn, who visited Lee in Hong Kong in late 1972, "spun in the blender, running seven miles a day. His skin was like very thin velvet—you could see every muscle, and every muscle, of course, was absolutely workable. It was like he could leap twenty feet in the air and stick on the wall and come down. That shining glowing velvet skin. He looked beautiful."

I am all styles; yet I am no style. "I use no way as way, have no limitation as limitation," said Lee.

Bruce Lee was movie star, writer, stunt choreographer, director, producer, philosopher, marketing genius, revolutionary, fighting innocent, little man's messiah. In his quest to become the complete person—warrior and healer, monk and lover, creature of intellect and of flesh and of spirit—he felt the need to be the best in the world at almost everything he undertook.

Then, something began to go terribly, inexplicably wrong.

*   *   *

Death of the Dragon script, page 67:

> WE SEE: *Lee removing his shirt before his fight with Chuck Norris in* Way of the Dragon: *there's an aura around him; he glows with the certainty of his own invulnerability.*

> NEXT, WE SEE: *Lee less than six months later, in the opening fight from* Enter the Dragon, *the last scene filmed for the movie. His skin looks stretched tight and he moves stiffly, mechanically. He's a figure in an El Greco painting—angular, elongated, ready to ascend into heaven.*

Twenty-three

B Y MID-1972, Lee was being featured prominently in almost every issue of Hong Kong's numerous daily newspapers. Says Wall, "Wherever we were driving, they'd scream, they'd wave and squeal. It reminded me of clips I'd seen of Muhammad Ali and Elvis Presley getting mobbed. It was unbelievable, it was overwhelming."

To prevent riots, department stores closed to allow Lee to shop by himself. When he wanted to go for a drive to relax, he was escorted by motorcycle police. It was a by-product of Lee's martial training to be purposely paranoid. For years he'd worked at being aware of movements of people who might attack him, to size up everyone in crowds. The eminently self-actualized Bruce Lee's martial fanaticism did not prepare him for the noose of hyper-celebrity in an enormously crowded, very small city.

In early 1971, when he was living in Los Angeles, Lee had weighed better than 145 pounds. By late 1972 he was down to 126; in May 1973, his doctor says, he was at 122. Lee said that he'd purposely dropped weight, that lowering his percentage of body fat made him appear more muscular on-screen. "Look at me," he told Hollywood student Ted Wong, who visited him in

Hong Kong. "Nothing but muscle and bones. I feel good, I'm strong."

"Bruce's body must have been less than one percent fat," says Dr. Donald Langford, the Lee family's physician in Hong Kong. "It was obscene how little body fat he had."

In the States, Lee had been playful and jovial: "a joker and a cut-up," says Coburn; "a clown," says Jabbar. In Los Angeles, Lee had played practical jokes on friends; he'd laughed often and easily. In Hong Kong the unexpected pressures of fame left him insecure, tense, easily agitated.

"He became very paranoid," Coburn says sadly. "He had this impenetrable aura, this shield around him for ten, maybe twelve feet. Anybody who came within that area was real suspect and they had to watch out."

Since his Hollywood days, Lee had been an occasional "recreational" drug user. Now, in hopes of calming himself and relieving the choking level of stress he felt that he was under, he regularly ate hashish brownies and leaves of marijuana. In Hong Kong he chose not to smoke the drugs, not wanting to damage his health.

He suffered greater paranoia, sleeplessness, memory loss. And headaches. He feuded with Coburn and Silliphant; sniped at McQueen, at co-workers, at fans, at "ignorant" Hong Kong Chinese in general; after an accident in which his hand was severely cut, he threatened to kill Bob Wall on an *Enter the Dragon* set. "He was repeating himself," says Wall, sympathetically. "He told me a story on the phone, then I went to his place and he told me the story twice more, every time like he'd never said it before. It was clear that there was something wrong. I thought he was just plain overworked. But he was concerned. You could see he was concerned."

Coburn laments the ways Lee changed in Hong Kong. "He used to express so much joy. You know, that's a hard thing to express. For a man, anyway. Sometimes it happens in a woman. Bruce could arouse that joy in me. But that's the thing that had left. That left before he left."

Ever since moving to Hong Kong, Lee had sent regular reports of his astounding successes to his former student Ted Ashley at Warner Brothers. Fred Weintraub flew to Hong Kong to meet Lee on the set of *Game of Death*. In the fall of 1972, Lee and Weintraub signed contracts. Bruce Lee would get that for which he had striven for so long: he would make his first film for international audiences and would become a global star.

The proposed title of the picture was *Blood and Steel*, which Lee fought hard to change to *Enter the Dragon*—to signify his arrival. He stopped work on *Game of Death* to begin production of *Enter the Dragon*.

"I feel a power bubbling up inside me," he said. It is this power—a beautiful lunacy—that we see roll from Lee in his *Enter the Dragon* fights.

"Bruce was very in touch with his own personal octane," exclaims Jabbar, who worked with Lee on several fights for *Game of Death*. "He could be there at the edge and he could get right to it. Bruce'd be white-hot in less than three-quarters of a second."

"*Intense* is the first word that comes to mind," says *Enter the Dragon* co-producer Paul Heller, when asked to describe Lee on the set. "He could focus himself at any one thing more totally than anybody. He was more alive than anybody I've ever seen. His body—you could press and it was like hitting a piece of mahogany—there was no give anywhere."

"That boy is crankin'," an LSD-stoned dorm-mate of mine said in September 1973 while staring hang-jawed at Lee in one of his more orgasmic *Enter the Dragon* battles.

Intense. Alive. White-hot. Crankin'. No give.

His best friend, James Lee, died in Oakland; Yip Man passed away in Hong Kong. Director Robert Clouse's wife claims that during the filming of *Enter the Dragon* Lee told her that he would be dead before his next birthday.

Principal photography for *Enter the Dragon* was completed in April 1973. Lee edited fight scenes and dubbed his voice to the soundtrack, and went back to work on *Game of Death*. He'd become regarded as a mystically empowered fighter, and was challenged through Hong Kong newspapers, as well as on the streets, by would-be usurpers.

Tales of these duels are no less the stuff of myth than are the theories about his death. An often-told legend (perhaps originating, as many such fables did, with Alex Ben Block's 1974 quickie biography, *The Legend of Bruce Lee*) has it that as a guest on *Enjoy Yourself Tonight,* upstart Lee was noisily beckoned by an elderly kung-fu master to try to push him out of his strongest fighting stance. According to the story, Lee rose from his seat, sauntered across the stage, and punched the old man in the face. In Bruce Lee folklore, the ancient master was knocked flat on the seat of his trousers. "I don't push," Lee reportedly said by way of explanation, "I punch." It would seem to be a perfect jeet kune do thesis. There is, however, no film to confirm that this "televised" exchange took place. And no one I've been able to find who worked on *Enjoy Yourself Tonight* remembers it. What's more, regardless of everything happening in his life, Lee, who was not so much a "bad guy" as he was just very young and stressed out, and impulsively younger than his age, would have had little reason to flatten some crotchety old man.

Fog and shadows.

"It was like *Gunfight at the OK Corral*," claims Heller of Lee's encounters. "They stand and tap their foot and you've got to take up the challenge. And Bruce would ignore it or walk away. Sometimes he couldn't. These were fierce encounters and the guys would get *hurt*. Bruce was so fast—he had reflexes and timing I defy anybody to this day to match."

Mist and dreams.

Although almost all tales of Lee's Hong Kong battles have little more substance than television legends about Billy the Kid, it's true that newspaper ads offered movie contracts to the challenger who could dethrone the seemingly invincible Bruce Lee. Lee was involved in a couple of real skirmishes. He side-kicked a hair stylist who challenged him on a *Fist of Fury* set, and thumped two fistically ambitious stunt extras while *Enter the Dragon* was being filmed. More seriously, one aspiring kung-fu hero apparently leaped the stone wall that enclosed Lee's Kowloon Tong home. Upon landing, he was afforded the uncommon privilege of getting folded by the right foot of Hong Kong's most legendary kick fighter, then tossed from the property.

Lee student Herb Jackson says, "This fella said to Bruce, 'How good are you?' And Bruce was popping mad. 'This guy invading my home, my own private home,' he told me. Bruce said he side-kicked this guy harder than he'd ever kicked anyone. He gave it all to him."

Gave it all. Lee, who signed Hong Kong fan photos, "Peace and Love, Bruce Lee," kept a black velvet poster above his desk in the study in his house. In the poster, two cartoon vultures are perched atop a dead tree. "Patience, hell," one vulture says to the other. "I'm gonna kill somethin'."

Lee had become the only star coveted by studios all over the globe: Warner Brothers, which had shunned him less than eighteen months before, hoped to sign him to star in several films; Paramount wanted him, as did Italian, Taiwanese, and other Hong Kong moviemakers.

Another reason Lee felt suffocated was that he had promoted Bruce Lee as the single deadliest human on the planet: he was sure that he would eventually have to support this claim. The world's chief exponent of unarmed combat bought a handgun (all firearms were illegal in Hong Kong), which he carried with him when he left his house.

On May 10, while at Golden Harvest dubbing his voice for *Enter the Dragon,* Lee collapsed and was rushed to a hospital, near death. He suffered a series of full-body seizures and cerebral edema. It was the next day before he regained full consciousness.

In the first week of June, the worried Lee flew to UCLA Medical Center for further tests. His mother and brother now lived in Los Angeles. He stopped by the apartment they shared.

"He said he was wondering how much he could push his body," says younger brother Robert. "He's constantly pushing himself to higher levels. He's always out to find more knowledge. He said, 'Oh, man, the doctor told me I got a body like an eighteen-year-old.' And he was thin but he was in good spirits."

Lee also spoke with James Coburn. "'They told me I was in perfect shape, everything is cool. Just take it easy. Just take it easy for a while,'" Coburn quotes Lee as saying.

Upon returning to Hong Kong, Lee quit physical training, except for daily runs through his neighborhood, and concentrated his energies on his movie career.

Six weeks later, on the twentieth of July, 1973, three weeks before the release of *Enter the Dragon,* Bruce Lee died.

Section Five

RIDING THE GHOST TRAIN

I have on my table a violin string. It is free.
I twist one end of it and it responds. It is free.
But it is not free to do what a violin string
is to do—produce music.

So I take it, fix it in my violin and
tighten it until it is taut.
Only then is it free
to be a violin string.

—RABINDRANATH TAGORE

Twenty-four

WITHIN HOURS, Linda Lee issued a statement that her husband had inexplicably collapsed while taking a walk with her in the meditation garden outside their home. On the twenty-fifth of July, 25,000 people attended Lee's funeral, the largest in Hong Kong's history. His body was flown to the United States for a second funeral; pallbearers included McQueen and Coburn. Among others, Coburn and Ashley delivered eulogies. He was quietly buried in Seattle's Lakeview Cemetery, near Linda's mother's home.

Enter the Dragon was released the second Friday in August.

On the basis of that one picture, Bruce Lee became a worldwide celebrity. Japanese teenagers cut their hair like his. Taiwanese eulogized him as "Man with the Golden Singing Legs." Thousands of martial-arts schools sprouted up across Britain, Europe, and the United States. Hundreds upon hundreds of fan magazines were published with fictionalized accounts of Lee's heroic deeds. Bruce Lee comic books and cartoons were produced and released in Asia. The chief lyric and title of a hot disco song in India was "Here's to That Swell Guy, Bruce Lee." Tens of millions of people came to see Lee's movie fights as virtual religious artifacts.

Internationally, *Enter the Dragon* was Warner Brothers' highest grossing movie of 1973. A theater in Iran played the film daily until January 1979, when Shah Pahlavi was overthrown by the Ayatollah Khomeini. Elvis bought a 35-millimeter copy of the movie and watched it dozens and dozens of times; inspired, he decided that he would finance, produce, and write his own martial-arts film, which began production but was never completed. During the 1970s, *Enter the Dragon* was released again and again in the United States; each time, it landed among the top-five-grossing pictures of the week. For nearly ten years, in major cities around the world, inner-city gang members turned out for *Enter the Dragon* with a ritualistic reverence similar to that of Catholics attending mass. As of the twenty-fifth anniversary of Lee's death, including worldwide video and television sales, *Enter the Dragon* had grossed over $400 million and had been listed, for more than twenty years, as one of the forty most profitable movies in the history of cinema.

*   *   *

On the day of Lee's Hong Kong funeral, the *South China Morning Post,* Hong Kong's largest English-language newspaper, disclosed that he had died, not with his wife, but in the apartment of movie actress Betty Ting Pei, with whom he'd been having an affair.

At a quickly arranged inquest, Ting Pei testified that when Lee came to her apartment, he complained of a headache; she gave him a tablet of a prescription medication called Equagesic, the ingredients of which are 200 milligrams of a common antianxiety agent (meprobamate) and 325 milligrams of aspirin. After swallowing the tablet, Lee left Ting Pei and went to lie on her bed; when she tried to wake him, he couldn't be roused. A University of London professor of forensic medicine, R. D. Teare, who supervised the inquest jury, determined the immediate cause of death to be cerebral edema: Lee's brain had become dramatically swollen and had pressed against the inside of his skull. Invariably, the pain from such a death is excruciating.

Among other released findings—Lee had eaten cannabis not only on the day of his death, but shortly before his May 10 collapse. Professor Teare said that although there was no evidence that Lee had been murdered, his death appeared not to be from natural causes. He concluded that Lee's demise was not accidental but was, instead, a "death by misadventure." Teare and the inquest jury concluded that edema had been caused by hypersensitivity to one or more of the ingredients in a single tablet of Equagesic.

Twenty-five

"Y ou'd almost have to use a Ouija board to come by that conclusion," says Dr. Donald Langford, a former Baptist missionary and Lee's physician in Hong Kong.

"This man was muscled like a squirrel, spirited as a horse. I've never seen anybody as physically fit as Bruce. Equagesic is prescribed in the million-dose range every day in Asia. Nobody dies from one tablet of Equagesic. No analgesic killed Bruce.

"In my opinion, the cause of Bruce Lee's death is obvious. Every time I saw him after May 10, he was further and further into his own hype. I don't think that Bruce thought that there was anybody in the world who knew what was good for him except Bruce Lee. That's what killed him. The same series of events that took place in May caused Bruce Lee's death in July. Bruce was particularly sensitive to one or more of the alkaloids in cannabis. He died from hypersensitivity to chemicals in cannabis or a cannabis by-product. Bruce's was a self-inflicted, though innocent, fatal illness."

Twenty-six

D R. PETER WU, the respected neurosurgeon who saved Lee's life in May, agrees. "I think that Bruce was fully convinced he was invincible, that he was immortal. This is what brought him down.

"He would have died in May from severe brain edema," says Dr. Wu, who is renowned for his cerebral edema research in Asian males. "Bruce was in a very critical condition. It was sheer luck that experienced medical people were available to help him. We removed quite a lot of hashish from his stomach. In Nepal there have been all kinds of neurological problems associated with hashish, especially cerebral edema. Bruce said that he was chewing the hashish because he was under a lot of pressure. Doing that, he would be exposed to all of the chemicals full-strength. We gave Bruce a long talk before he was discharged from hospital, asking him not to eat the stuff again. We told him that his very low percentage of body fat could make him vulnerable to drugs. We said that the effects would be heightened by continued contact. We also told him that his level of stress could dramatically magnify the effects. Since he'd already had a very bad time with the drug, we told him that the effects were likely to be worse next time.

"He said that it was harmless. He said that Steve McQueen had introduced him to it and Steve McQueen would not take it if there was anything bad about it. I asked him if Steve McQueen was a medical authority. He didn't get my joke.

"To tell the truth, when Bruce left hospital, I thought that he would be back. I had a very bad feeling about it."

Twenty-seven

WHY HAVEN'T THESE OPINIONS and this information been previously reported? Why wasn't hypersensitivity to cannabis part of the official verdict of the inquest jury?

"You have to understand something about Hong Kong Chinese culture," explains Dr. Langford. "When Bruce's body was wheeled into the emergency room, all the Chinese vanished. It was difficult to find anyone to take care of him. The Chinese weren't about to be connected with, to be blamed for, the death of Hong Kong's most famous hero. It would have been regarded as a terrible loss of face.

"The same is true of the inquest: people weren't about to step up and say that Bruce Lee had died from eating cannabis or some related product. At the beginning of the inquest proceedings, Dr. Wu and a couple of other doctors and I were pulled to the side and asked to play down the role of cannabis in Bruce's death.

"For years, I was suspicious that this might have been some sort of cover-up. Now I realize that it was something else: they simply wanted to present a socially acceptable explanation. There was no recorded incidence of this drug as a cause of death. Hong Kong authorities felt that Bruce Lee's death had put them on the world stage. They were trying to avoid embarrassment, trying not to look silly. They didn't know that no one was watching. No one cared about Bruce Lee. Amazingly, not one single Hong Kong reporter—or any reporter anywhere—ever interviewed me about Bruce or his death."

Twenty-eight

WHEN LEE DIED, he was not wealthy. He left a wife and two young children with one obvious means of financial support: two six-figure life insurance policies.

He'd signed statements, when he'd taken out the policies in 1972, that he'd never used any form of illegal drug.

Joe Lewis says, "Hell, back in Hollywood, I saw Bruce doing dope right in front of me. One time, he walked into my place and started passing out these huge joints the size of big cigars. I said, 'Bruce, that's not the way you do it. You just roll one little one and pass it all around.' He tells me, 'No need to share. I want everybody to have their own.' And he thumps his chest like he did in the movies, real big and proud. Everybody thought that was funny. That was Bruce, all right. Bruce to a T. But it's not like anybody thought that anything was wrong with all that. It was the sixties and seventies. We thought it was innocent. Everybody was doing drugs."

Coburn confirms Lee's Hollywood drug use. "He'd want to get high and have a ball, listen to music. Blowing Gold was one of his favorite things."

And Wall tells this story: "I was in Bruce's study in Hong Kong while we were making *Enter the Dragon*. He kept the door to that room locked when he wasn't there. He had this plate of pot brownies sitting on the desk and while we're talking he kept eating brownies and offering them to me."

Lewis remembers another Lee anecdote he regards as significant. "There was this time in about 1969 that Bruce was at the house and my wife fixed him a drink. Some kind of sweet, syrupy thing. I don't remember what it was called, I don't drink. And Bruce drank it and then he got unbelievably sick. He turned red, he was sweating, sweat was running all down his face. And we helped him to the bathroom. He threw up and threw up and then threw up still more. It doesn't seem like such a mystery to me how Bruce died. Some people are just real sensitive to what they put in their bodies. And Bruce was one of those guys."

* * *

Donald and Mary Langford lived in the same Kowloon Tong neighborhood as the Bruce Lee family, "less than fifty yards from their estate," says Langford.

"Somewhere around midnight on the night that Bruce died, Raymond Chow called. He was leaving the hospital with Linda, he said. He asked if they could stop by my house.

"When they got there about one o'clock, Linda was distraught. She didn't know what to do, what to tell reporters. This is a young, inexperienced woman who loved her husband and was enormously proud of him. He was becoming a big movie star and he was incredibly fit. She had no reason to believe that she wouldn't have many, many years to spend with Bruce.

"Now there's this. Not only is he dead, but here she is with all these questions about this actress he died with. What's more, she has two children to take care of—by herself. And she's in Hong Kong where she can barely speak the language. Linda and I were in the same Cantonese class for Americans. She struggled with the language even more than I did.

"That night, in my living room, she asked what I knew about Bruce's relationships with women, whether or not he was a philanderer. I told her truthfully, to the best of my knowledge, that he had no other relationships. But Linda thought, quite accurately, that the Hong Kong press would devour her husband. Her major concern was how to keep tawdry things from being said. She handled herself with considerable poise and dignity during those times. I don't think that anyone could've done better than she did. I believe it was in my living room that she and Raymond Chow decided what statement they'd give to reporters.

"Personally, I'd have considerable sympathy for Linda if I knew she fictionalized an aspect or two of Bruce's demise, not only to protect his hero's image, but to get the money she felt was rightfully hers to raise those kids."

*   *   *

In 1974 the two companies from which Bruce Lee had purchased life insurance wrote checks to Linda Lee for half of the face value of those policies. And she sold all rights and royalties from *Enter the Dragon* to Raymond Chow for a nominal fee.

In the years following Lee's passing, his reputation as a martial artist became badly damaged not only by fictionalized pulp magazine and paperback book accounts, and of course by Chopalong Wong imitators (many people believe that Bruce Li—whose real name is Ho Chun Tao—is Bruce Lee and that, instead of four movies, Lee made dozens), but by his own students.

The year before his death, Lee closed his Los Angeles, Seattle, and San Francisco schools and demanded that his art not be taught by the three "authorized" jeet kune do instructors, Dan Inosanto in Los Angeles, James Lee in Oakland, and Taky Kimura in Seattle, or by any of Lee's other pupils.

George Tan explains Lee's motives: "He felt that no one was qualified. A lot of people who hung out with Bruce, especially during his Hollywood years, were weak men, first-class wimps. Most of his students were guys he could use as moving, breathing punching bags. The exception was Jimmy Lee—but he died before Bruce. Bruce knew that the lack of quality in his students and teaching could come back to haunt him."

With Lee's death and the success of *Enter the Dragon,* former students, most of whom wanted honestly to perpetuate Lee's teaching methods, also recognized that considerable money could be made by claiming to be heirs to Lee's art. Says Tan, "Bruce knew that this would happen. It's like Christianity or most any other thing. First, along comes an innovator. He dies and the guys left behind are followers. Most of them don't have any real idea what Bruce was saying or doing, let alone the ability to execute it."

In the post-Lee years, jeet kune do has become much of what Lee sought to change in the martial arts: it pretends to be free-flowing, but is structured, systematic, formulaic, unintentionally worshipful, paralyzingly dogmatic. "Lots of these JKD people sit around and play office politics," Tan says, "fighting each other for the money they can make marketing Bruce's bones as icons. Bruce was a revolutionary. He did his best to knock down the whole office building and grind up the bones of everybody inside. He's the guy who wanted to take a wrecking ball to the very *idea* of having an office building."

Lewis agrees. "If Bruce knew what some of these guys were teaching and calling JKD, he'd claw his way out of his grave to kick their shiny behinds. The jeet kune do crew has become a bigger bunch of pussies than any group I know of in the martial arts. Jeet kune do, my foot. *Geek* kune do is more like it. You try that stuff in a real fight, against real tough guys, you're gonna get yourself hurt bad."

*   *   *

On the thirty-first of March 1993, approaching the twentieth anniversary of Lee's death, his only son, Brandon Bruce Lee, was shot on a movie set in Wilmington, North Carolina. He died that evening and was buried beside his father in Seattle. The .44-caliber handgun with which the younger Lee was shot was supposed to have contained blanks. It was the first time in the history of film that a leading actor had been shot and killed by a live round on the set.

The younger Lee had wanted to admire his father, but had difficulty separating the myths he had heard from the breathing human being he had only briefly known. After his father's death, Brandon Lee was regularly challenged by schoolmates who'd learned that he was the son of Bruce Lee. "Back then, we moved around a lot," he said. "I'd get to a new school and there'd always be somebody there trying to kick my ass."

Brandon Lee had not wanted to perform martial art or to make action movies. He studied drama at Emerson College in Boston and took acting lessons in Manhattan in hope of becoming a serious actor, but had little success getting roles, and eventually chose to take advantage of his unique heritage. He decided to jump-start an acting career by making a few martial arts movies; he believed that the success he'd find in those would allow him the opportunity to perform in quality dramatic projects both on the screen and on stage.

By early 1993, Brandon Lee had starred in one martial-arts movie for a Hong Kong studio and two action features for American producers. He had multiple-picture deals with 20th Century Fox and with Carolco Studios. The younger Lee was hard at work on his fourth film—the adult Bruce Lee, of course, completed four movies in which he was the star. Brandon had nearly finished work on his first vehicle for Carolco Studios, *The Crow*. His role was that of a pop idol who has been resurrected to avenge his own murder. The scene being filmed when Brandon was shot was one in which his character is killed. It's not a dissimilar plot to many of the exploitation films about his father.

Legendary rumors about the father's death seemed ready-baked for the son's. (Crows are symbols of death in both the East and the West. Some Chinese are superstitious about the word *death* being used in titles. One of the fables about the elder Lee's

demise was that the gods—or fate or karma or *something*—
killed him for naming his work-in-progress *Game of Death*.)
The seeming relationships between the deaths of Bruce and
Brandon Lee caused greater confusion about the elder Lee's
exit; details became blurred, intertwined. Many people came to
remember Bruce Lee as having been shot and murdered.

Within weeks of Brandon Lee's death, the son's story had
become a footnote to the father's legend.

*   *   *

In 1993 and 1994, at public auctions, Linda Lee sold many of
Bruce Lee's personal items, including his business cards, his
tank tops and leather jacket, his wallet, his platform shoes. She
gave the money from these sales to charities.

Among the few items that did not sell were the only substantive ones on the block: Lee's handwritten notes and
anatomical drawings for the fight scenes in *Way of the Dragon*,
the screen bouts into which he put the most work and those
with which he was most pleased.

"I was teaching this seminar at a karate school in Ohio," says
Lewis. "The instructor had this pair of Bruce Lee's yellow sneakers—you know, the ones he wore in *Game of Death* ("completed" by Raymond Chow, with a Lee imitator, in 1977)—that
he brings out and holds up in front of the students.

"In traditional karate schools, at the beginning of class, students bow to a Buddhist shrine. This guy's students bowed to
these little yellow shoes. And then this teacher talks about the
aura he feels around the shoes and leans over and tells me

that his students will get proper martial energy from these old size 7 Cs.

"I found out the funniest thing later. This guy didn't know that those sneakers weren't Bruce's. They were ones made for a Bruce Lee imitator after Bruce was dead."

Twenty-nine

BEFORE THE NAME BRUCE LEE is entirely enveloped by the mists of pop mythology, perhaps it would be useful to define what the person who breathed and fought and dreamed and died has left us.

Lee was the Frank Lloyd Wright of martial art. He obsessively studied what had come before him, then reinvented the rules, in the hope of creating a universal, interconnected fighting (non)form. Lee's martial art was as distinct as Wright's "organic architecture," if not as roundly developed. (But then, Wright lived to be a very old man who'd worked on his art for many decades.) In only a few years Lee revolutionized Asian fighting disciplines, made them "organically" American, and evangelized this product around the globe.

It's hard to overstate how visible the martial disciplines have become because of Lee. If he had not existed, few of us would have heard of martial art or kung-fu. Before Lee's death, there were fewer than five hundred martial-arts schools in the world; by the late 1990s, because of his influence, there were more than 20 million martial-arts students in the United States alone.

"There isn't a martial artist on the planet who hasn't been influenced by Bruce," George Tan claims. And this seeming overstatement is probably true.

"Karate people all over the globe are light-years farther along than when Bruce was alive," Lewis declares. "For instance, a lot of guys in this country call the martial art they practice 'American freestyle.' That way of thinking exists because of Bruce. He helped a whole lot of people jump out of some small boxes."

In addition to Lee's considerable legacy of having introduced more Westerners to Asian culture and philosophy than anyone else in history, he foreshadowed, and was a forebear of, the hyperfitness body culture of the latter portion of our century. Before Lee, few of us had seen anyone with his streamlined, super-functional, no-scrap muscularity. *How can anyone look like that?* I wondered, watching *Enter the Dragon;* in 1999, studying photos of him on my desk, it still seems almost impossible. Yet this aesthetic, first encountered in Lee, has since become not only desirable but is regarded as a twenty-first-century, new-evolutionary goal, among both men and women.

What's more, Lee fundamentally changed movie fight scenes: those of us born before 1960 grew up in a culture that considered kicking to be "dirty" fighting; martial arts are now employed in nearly every fight in almost every action movie.

The best, and most successful, martial-arts movie personality since Lee has been, of course, Jackie Chan, who, as a stuntman, had the distinction of being anonymously killed by Lee in both *Fist of Fury* and *Enter the Dragon.* Chan's on-screen comic kung-fu genius/doofus persona was derived by Hong Kong pro-

ducers partly from Lee's Tang Loong ("China Dragon") character in *Way of the Dragon,* far and away Lee's most popular
movie in Asia. But no one, including Chan, has come close to
re-creating the verisimilitude, dramatic pacing, and resonance
of Lee's fights. What we've been left with post-Lee are such
de-evolutionized by-products as Teenage Mutant Ninja Turtles,
Power Rangers, Steven Seagal, Jean-Claude Van Damme, and
Sylvester Stallone, who patterned not only *Rocky* boxing
scenes but *Rambo*'s hypertrophic gunplay displays on Lee's
movie battles.

And, more surprisingly than his influence on other movie
and television stars, if there had not been Bruce Lee movies,
there might not have been a "Sugar" Ray Leonard.

In the late 1980s, when I was finally able to begin making a
writing career for myself, three of the first four assignments I
received from national magazines were about Leonard. As I got
the opportunity to spend time with him, Ray and I found that we
had some things in common. When we were kids, we'd both collected comics by the hundreds. As adolescents, we'd worked to
emulate Ali and Lee, and we were still big fans. After we became
friendly, I mailed Ray several videocassettes of rare Lee footage
that George Tan had sent me. When we spent time together, Ray
and I often spoke about martial arts and discussed a couple of
little-known facts about the foundation of his ring skills: Ray said
that he learned much of his defense from watching Lee in movies;
and, as Leonard trained for fights, during sparring rounds he
often imitated Lee's alleycat-in-heat battle cries.

Writing a profile of Ray for the *Washington Post Magazine*
before one of his final bouts, I interviewed him after a training

session. "Davis, I hope you brought some Bruce stuff with you," was the first thing he said as I took a seat on an old yellow sofa in his dressing room.

I said I had a tape in the car.

"Hey, man, I'll let you in on something I've never told anybody," he said, taking a seat beside me. "When I was a kid, I used to come back from Bruce movies and go into my mom's backyard. He fired me up so much I took my fist and drove it into the ground until I made a hole three or four inches deep." He didn't look embarrassed by his admission.

I unabashedly told him that I had done things like that, too.

Numerous other world-champion boxers have been inspired by Lee, including Mike Tyson, who buys hundreds of martial-arts movies and, like Leonard, has said that he learned explosiveness from watching Lee in *Enter the Dragon*. It's a lesson that hasn't always served Tyson well.

And there's Hector "Macho" Camacho. "I got an Elvis room and a Bruce Lee room in my house," Camacho reveals, "with posters and pictures everywhere." When Camacho is club-hopping, I've seen him sport white traditional Chinese garb modeled on what Lee wore in *Fist of Fury*.

And, at age fifteen, influenced by Lee, southpaw defensive phantom Wilfredo Benitez became the youngest-ever world champion pugilist. Benitez's nickname was "The Dragon." He's the fighter from whom Leonard won his first world title. On that day in the ring, with big lights playing across their gleaming faces, torsos, arms, and legs, Leonard and Benitez seemed mirror images of each other.

*   *   *

In addition to inspiring professional athletes, Lee has influenced the way every single action-movie hero and heroine has moved in fights since the mid-1970s. And he has inspired video-game programmers and stunt guys. "Almost all stunt coordinators who came after Bruce were influenced," says Tan. "Any movie or TV show with fights in it—*Raiders of the Lost Ark, Star Wars, Buffy the Vampire Slayer, The Matrix,* animated fights in *The Lion King*—it doesn't matter what. If you know what you're looking at, you'll catch camera angles and martial-arts techniques from Bruce's scenes, stuff Bruce invented. He contributed so much to the industry that has never been recognized."

But did Lee make a significant contribution to anything more ennobling than the (rather sociopathic) prettification of violence?

Perhaps the best, most life-affirming, of that which Lee left us is this: a popularization of forward-looking art and philosophy.

When asked why he removed rear windows from automobiles he purchased and replaced them with sheets of metal, Frank Lloyd Wright answered, "I don't look behind me." It is a statement that I believe Bruce Lee would have admired.

"What we're doing is sort of musical jeet kune do," says electric bass reinventor Victor Wooten of Béla Fleck and the Flecktones. The body of Wooten's custom-designed instrument is emblazoned with a porcelain black-and-white yin-yang symbol. Inspired by Lee, Wooten has studied wing chun and other martial disciplines since his teen years; he often wears Bruce Lee T-shirts on stage. He and his brother, the pyrotechnic percussionist for the Flecktones, Roy "Futureman" Wooten, both consider Lee to be among their major musical and spiritual mentors. They say that they learned much about complex rhythms they eventually used in their music by growing up watching Lee and his movies.

Where Lee integrated fighting forms of the world into his art, the compositions that the multiple Grammy Award–winning Flecktones compose and play are informed by such formerly disparate sources as R&B, classical, jazz, bluegrass, Celtic, and Cajun; and by Middle Eastern, East Indian, Chinese, Japanese, and American folk. "No way as way," says Roy "Futureman" Wooten, winking.

As was true of the martial art that Lee developed, Flecktone tunes are at once simple *and* complex, substantive and very accessible. This music is playfully American, yet international—and, to many people, including me, profoundly cosmic. And it is played with a majesty that, like Lee's on-screen performances, can seem beyond the capacity of normal human beings.

Banjoist Béla Fleck explains his art without explaining it away. "You can't name what we do," he says, implying something tantamount to the spiritual. "To us, this is life. We just write and play the music."

To me, Fleck, the Wootens, and their music verify that there's little that's unique about "Bruce Lee's" philosophy. Arguably, "Lee's" organic ideas are the major working theory of art over the past hundred years. And, as has been true for artisans from Monet to Wright to Miles Davis to Fleck and to novelist Tom Robbins (who studies martial art in Seattle with Lee student Jim DeMile), this non-way of approaching art and life seems as much biological as consciously controlled by people: it arrived in the world as if by osmosis.

*   *   *

Among other "biological" movements in which Lee had a role: the post–World War II Western ideal of the superior Christian, Anglo-Saxon, mannerly tough guy (*á la* Duke Wayne and Rocky Marciano). Humbled by the Koreans, crippled by Ali, and resolutely de-limbed by the Viet Cong, this bad old white boy was killed dead, and replaced in the public consciousness, by little bitty Bruce Lee.

As millions of tiny twits like me—whether we were yellow, black, white, or brown—first saw Lee on big, enveloping movie screens, we no longer felt so little, so powerless. Lee even managed to help a few of us swim out of our bowls of sad soup and find something resembling real dry-land lives.

Others, however, became still more enthralled.

In the late 1980s, one Bruce Lee fan mailed videocassettes to Linda Lee and several of Lee's former students in which, while throwing a series of round-kicks toward a video camera, he claimed to be the son of Lee and Lindsay *(The Bionic Woman)* Wagner, and then confessed his desire to "connect with" his "big brother Brandon" and "little sister Shannon." The Lees' family attorney sent notice to this fellow that he was not to approach Linda Lee or her children. He was last heard from in Seattle, where he'd changed his name to Dalton Lee (the name of the Patrick Swayze character in the 1980s action movie *Roadhouse*), and had moved to a motel near Bruce Lee's grave.

175

And there was Mikey Miyazaki, the son of a wealthy Tokyo businessman, who, in his early twenties, used his father's money to make his bedroom into a composite of several *Enter the Dragon* sets. For more than a decade, televisions were mounted to the ceiling in the room's corners, and Miyazaki perpetually played a different Lee movie on all four monitors and wore Lee-style Chinese garb for pajamas.

Then there's Blade Leong, who lived in L.A., claimed that he was Bruce Lee (after all, they shared the same initials), and made his wife dress like Linda Lee in the 1960s, down to her one-piece shifts and beehive hairstyle.

Another true believer was a retired Mongolian physician, Ichinorov Dendev, who, in the fall of 1993, in celebration of the twentieth anniversary of Lee's death, set off on a nine-month pilgrimage during which he and two disciples unsuccessfully attempted to walk across the Bering Straits from Mongolia to Seattle to place flowers on the grave of the god of martial art.

More infamously, a young Londoner sent letters to the British martial-arts publication *Kung-fu Monthly* (this magazine's unofficial motto: "All Lee, All the Time"), in which he tried to explain that the word *God* was an acronym for the movie *Game of Death*. He eventually hijacked a bus and rammed it through a shopfront, screaming, "I'm Bruce Lee, I'm God. I'm Bruce Lee, I'm God."

And there's the Elvis Presley and Bruce Lee acolyte in northern Idaho, who named his son Brandon, his daughters Shannon and Lisa Marie, and changed his own name to Jesus Lee Presley.

Then, on the twentieth of July, 1986, Betty Ting Pei gave birth to a son, who, she told friends, was the reincarnation of Bruce Lee.

*   *   *

I, too, have had a role in the proliferation of the Bruce Lee (non)gospel.

In addition to naming my son Isaac (as I wrote earlier in this book) *Lee* Miller—after my father, Roy Lee Miller, and Bruce Lee—I developed a documentary film and wrote a script about Lee for *Enter the Dragon* producer Fred Weintraub. (*Enter,* which was made for less than $600,000, made Weintraub self-sustainably wealthy.) During an early production meeting in his Century City office, despite having courted his newly contracted writer by regularly referring to himself as Lee's "dear friend," Weintraub said, "You have to understand, movies aren't art; they're commerce. I don't care about the truth of this putz's life. You don't have to exactly say he was fuckin' Marilyn Monroe—but you better damn well imply it."

Badly needing the money, and still passionately committed to doing the best work about Lee that I had in me, I stayed with Weintraub's project. (Although much of what I found over the following months was less than ennobling, I well understand that if someone were to view my own life through any sort of reverential binoculars, it would not hold up well.) In addition to writing the script for Weintraub's feature, I worked unofficially as researcher, facilitator, interviewer, and line producer. The story that I developed was apparently more to my liking than Weintraub's. Although I received sole screen credit for Fred's show, hardly a word I wrote was used in the film. Weintraub's co-producer in this project was Tom Kuhn, the former Warner executive for whom Lee had auditioned for the starring role in the *Kung Fu* TV series.

I called my script *Death by Misadventure: The Mysterious Life of Bruce Lee*. Admittedly, not a great title. Weintraub's and Kuhn's show, however, was released under the thoroughly dubious name *Curse of the Dragon*.

Thirty

1

BRUCE LEE WAS THE progenitor of postmodern martial art. The two questions I'm most often asked about him are, How did he die? and, How good was he as a martial artist?

Well, as best I can tell, he was plenty wonderful. Probably the best martial practitioner of his time. Does this make him the best fighter in the world, then or ever? Was he the real, live, twentieth-century god of martial art?

This is some of what we know: Bruce Lee was blessed with good long arms (Dan Inosanto says, "Bruce had the reach of a six-footer"), incredible initiation speed and reaction time, and he hit big-hard compared to others in the Asian "fighting" disciplines. "Bruce had phenomenal attributes," confirms Joe Lewis. "Amazing speed, power, strength, reflexes."

Says Hayward Nishioka, "He was the quickest person I've ever seen. In that area he was king. And he knew it. He had that same cockiness Americans have. Americans say, 'I'm arrogant, and I'll show you why. I can do it. I'm good.'"

World-class athlete Kareem Abdul Jabbar was more than a little impressed with Lee's prowess. "He had cunning, killer instinct, and the will to dominate. And incredible athletic skills:

balance, eye-hand coordination, timing. And all that driven by a very intense will."

Yet, regardless of fighting ability, numerous intangibles are required to be an outstanding warrior. Among these is proper anatomy. When I was trying to make a career as four-limbed lightning, it took me years to learn that there were many necessary biological qualities I didn't possess. I have the wrong-shaped chin, excess tissue over, under, and around both sad-dog eyes, terrible vision, and a long neck.

Lee had dramatic anatomical inadequacies, too, including a pointed chin, a narrow jaw, and a skinny neck; small bones, particularly his wrists and ankles; and horrible vision—very nearsighted, he couldn't see ten feet from his face without corrective lenses: It goes without saying that it's tough to get out of the way of fists and feet if you can't tell that they're being beamed at you. And, considering the circumstances of his death, as well as his physical stature, it seems reasonable to say that he may have been a markedly fragile human being.

Dissecting Lee's film battles also reveals that, although there's little doubt he understood and preached the necessity of coordinated offensive and defensive movement, and wanted to move beautifully, compared to boxers he was not a consummate mover: he was pretty good at in-and-out, forward-and-backward movements—he pranced instead of gliding, though, which sacrifices power while magnifying the effects of blows with which your opponent(s) catch you. And he had little idea how to effectively accomplish more-subtle side-to-side movements. Also, he often held his head high and stiff, though he understood the value of keeping it low, serpentine, and mobile.

As has been shown when martial-arts-trained fighters attempt to box professionally, their lack of lateral mobility and a general upper-body stiffness often help to sit them down hard on the seat of their jammies.

And, as is true of most guys in the martial disciplines, Lee was not street-rough. He was middle-class tough, at most. Not that there's anything wrong with this. Indeed, in lots of ways it's comforting to discover that Lee wasn't a hard-core tough guy. Like most of us, he was a person hoping and trying to cope, moment to moment, with the life that was presented to him.

Yet, if the way he treated his kind, timid wife and many of his students is an indication, some of his coping behavior was less than admirable.

"It was my birthday. And we're down at the studio," says Lee's friend and assistant instructor Dan Inosanto. "Bruce said, 'Dan, let's spar a little.' Then he turned that light switch of his on and suddenly it was a different person. He hit me one in the solar plex, one in the cheek. And I went down. I'm dazed, shaking my head—and he's laughing. He says, 'Bring out the birthday cake.' And he's singing 'Happy Birthday' and laughing. Bruce says, 'I just had to knock you out for your twenty-fourth birthday, Dan.' "

Lewis claims that there were numerous times he tried to get Lee to spar with him. "Bruce didn't spar anybody, except a couple of those guys who ran around sucking up to him. But there was one time he set me up. We're training and a couple of his students are standing around. He says, 'Joe, fire that forehand strike you're working on.' I fired it, he slipped it, and he said, 'Come on, Joe, do it again.' I did. And he says, 'Just once more, Joe.' The third time I fired the punch, he slipped it and came back with that triple punch you see right at the beginning of *Enter the Dragon*. He goes *ba-ba-bam*, fires the three shots, hits me square between the eyes. He suckered me. And it took him three tries to pull it off. Next thing I hear, his students are running around saying Bruce kicked my ass, completely showed me up. I'll tell you right now—I never, ever sparred with Bruce. It was never that open with Bruce, not once. Never the possibility of give and take, moment to moment, let's really get down and do it. Almost anybody, and I mean anybody, can make you look stupid setting you up like Bruce did me."

How do these stories relate to who Lee would have been as a fighter? They provide evidence that he was a bit of a bully. And what we're exploring when we evaluate Lee, as much as mechanics, is metaphysics. Bullies are often limited fighters who can be shocked out of their best stuff when they encounter willful opponents. "To whip a bully, you need to consistently break his spirit or have a stronger spirit," says Ray Leonard. "The important thing to beat any fighter is to whip him mentally and emotionally, to knock down his spirit and make him believe he can be stopped."

No doubt about it: Bruce Lee would have turned *my* scrawny little skin inside out and hung it on a coat rack. And surely he could have done the same with many famous movie-martial monkeys who arrived after his death. Yet Lee was untested as a fighter—and it isn't pointless to note that he seemed to prefer it that way. Who knows if he had the will to transcend his competition in those most feverish of battles, where willful fighters take your most stupendous shots and

keep coming at you—or sometimes simply smile at you. Everyone can be beaten, not just little writer-guys who've been
known to wear Bruce Lee T-shirts. And even Lee himself didn't
know whether he had the stuff it takes to keep going to the
well—to believe, after he brought up an empty bucket or two,
that he needed to keep going back.

2

Coburn: "That still pond he was always talking about. That
still pond in the middle of action, that pond deep inside. I don't
think he ever found that."

3

Jabbar: "Bruce wished he had more friends, but he didn't want
to be that vulnerable. He had to keep up a kind of mystique."

4

Coburn: "Wherever we were, he was always the center of
attention. He was always demonstrating his ability to control
people. And wherever he wasn't in control, he left."

5

"What's your style?" Bruce Lee is asked by an antagonist in
Enter the Dragon.

"You can call it 'the art of fighting without fighting,'" Lee
replies.

6

"He practices techniques and forms for years and years," said
Bruce Lee, "never knowing, always wondering, if he can defend

himself." To whom was the insightful movie-god of martial art referring?

7

Bruce Lee was possibly the first martial practitioner to have trained *as* a "scientific" fighter. Psychologically, he *needed* to be regarded—by himself and by others—as a fighter. These factors speak to Lee's motivation and commitment as a martial artist. But was he a *real* fighter?

"Angelo Dundee never fought," says Lewis, "but he understands the science of fighting. Robert DeNiro looks great as Jake LaMotta in *Raging Bull*. When he's standing in front of a mirror, he throws some good-looking punches, but he's still an actor, not a boxer. I must've heard Bruce say a hundred times, 'You can't swim without getting in the water, Joe.' But what Bruce did is he *thought* about sparring. Partly to make himself look good because he understood fighting, partly to look good in the movies. All the time standing on the shore watching other guys swim.

"People who do something over and over do it because they like it. Why do they like it? Because it empowers them, makes them feel special. Since Bruce wasn't fighting anybody who was good, why was it empowering to analyze all that karate and wrestling and boxing? If you're not gonna get in the ring and look good, then you want to *feel* good. And what's gonna make you feel good is when you know something—and people *believe* you know something. You want to understand Bruce Lee, what makes the boy tick. It's pretty simple—it's vanity, baby."

184

8

"Substitute the word 'swimmer' for 'fighter,'" says Lewis. "'This guy was the greatest *swimmer* of all time. He woulda beat everybody else, ever.'

"Was he?" I ask. "How many times did he win the Olympics?"

"'Aw, man, he didn't have to do all that.' That's what those JKD priests claim. 'He was *beyond* all that,' they say.

"Now here, this guy's never competed, never been to a swim meet, we've never seen him really swim. We don't even know how many swimming lessons he had, really. Do you see what I mean?

"Put another word in place of 'fighter,' does all of it start to sound stupid or what?"

9

How would little man's messiah Bruce Lee have done against *big* experienced tough guys of his time: Ali, Lewis (who was recently voted "Fighter of the Century" by fellow martial-arts competitors, and who in 1976 in their one—albeit playful— encounter, *immediately* had Ali tied up and powerless on the floor), Frazier, George Foreman, footballer Jim Brown, collegiate wrestler Dan Gable, show-wrestler Gorgeous George?

"Let's put it this way," says Lewis. "If 'Sugar' Ray Robinson, who was a helluva lot bigger than Bruce, got in a ring with Ali, his mainspring woulda got broke before his clock ever got wound. When big guys throw their best stuff, the wall-shakers, you can't believe how hard they hit. When they hit a little guy like Bruce, it could literally kill him."

10

Then there's one more, less celebrated bloke, among Lee's contemporaries, whose connection with Lee is worth noting.

"Without question, he's the toughest man of the century," says Chuck Norris. "And I'm not the only fella who feels that way."

Norris is referring not to his co-star in *Way of the Dragon,* but to seventy-year-old "Judo" Gene LeBell. For almost fifty years, LeBell has been a world-class *judoka* (as a 165-pound competitor, he won the overall national AAU championships in both 1954 and 1955; yes, he chumped the heavyweights), a world heavyweight wrestling champion, one of the most respected stuntfolks in television and movies (he launched his career as George Reeves's stunt double on the 1950s *Superman* TV series, and in the late 1990s he is still in demand) and a karate instructor.

LeBell began his education in personal combat as an aspiring pugilist. "My mother, Aileen Eaton, owned the Olympic Auditorium in Los Angeles," he says. "I grew up sparring guys like Ray Robinson and Archie Moore. I wanted to be a professional boxer, but my mother wouldn't let me. She said it was too rough, I'd get hurt. So that's when I began hangin' out with rasslers."

As he's speaking, LeBell is leaning back on a swivel chair behind the little maple desk in his workout cabin in the Santa Susana Mountains. He's barefoot; his long flat feet are stretched out in front of him and they're crossed atop his desk. He's medium-big, with a lopsided tough-guy smile and a shock of thin red hair that he combs straight back but that never seems to stay. His is not an untested face. LeBell's flattened countenance is reminiscent of a facial aesthetic most often encountered when watching Broderick Crawford movies. This afternoon he's wearing his idea of traditional training garb: a dramatically faded, torn, and threadbare black belt (the very same strap of material he's worn since the 1960s) and a mid-calf-length, pale *pink* gi.

"Mom knew rasslers were suave [he pronounces the word *swave*] and genteel," LeBell says, puffing himself up with feigned haughtiness. "She knew they wouldn't hurt little ol' me."

LeBell places his feet on the floor and stands. "From them, I learned to like to *stir-rettcchhh* people." He abruptly leans forward across his desk with eyes full-moon wide and mouth open in a "rassler's" growl; he moves his hands in front of his chest like he's milking a full-grown rhinoceros.

LeBell has "stir-rettcchhhed" lots of tough guys over the years, including Milo Savage in 1963, in the first ring contest to have featured a martial artist against a boxer. He's also stretched many of the world's best martial practitioners, including Norris, Lewis, and Stone.

"And about anybody else he's wanted to," Norris says.

"I was a stuntman on *The Green Hornet*," says LeBell. "Bruce was a hard guy to get to know, always actin' kinda sophisticated. So, when I got tired of it, I'd pick him up, sling him over my shoulder, and run all around the set with him. He'd scream, 'Put me down, put me down.' I reckon I teased him so much I eventually got him to loosen up a little. He got to where he took jokes pretty good—'specially if ya'd grabbed him 'round the neck."

Says Lewis of LeBell's encounters with the god of gung-fu: "When Gene squeezed him, Bruce'd make this high-pitched squeaking noise."

Thirty-one

WHEN LEE'S LIFE IS SERIOUSLY SCRUTINIZED, it becomes clear, almost immediately, that he was not who most of us have thought he was. He was neither a Ronald Wong-Donald at work in some chop-socky restaurant where feature flicks can be served up for corporate lunch money, nor was he an all-wise, mystically empowered ascetic.

Perhaps the highest compliment that Lee's own fans could pay him—and themselves—would be to look past the screen caricature, beyond the high-kicking clichés, to recognize some of the ways that he resembles each of us. As is true of Ali, one of the most important things that Lee has helped me see is this: Any and all notions that we have carried with us about him, are, at best, reductionist. (In other words, "deconstructive" journalism is inadequate to describe Lee or give us a real, "enlarging" sense of who he was.) And what's true for Lee applies to everyone: "I am human, and nothing human is foreign to me."

Unlike Bruce Lee's swaggering "I am all styles" fantasy, Terence's statement is not positivist, is not about work, about muscle strain; it's a declaration of his, and our, basic humanity. In nature, there's no such thing as paradox. There's only that which seems paradoxical. Though we may be uncomfortable with it, in many ways each of us is Mother Teresa *and* Jeffrey Dahmer, Gandhi and Hitler, Claude Debussy and Mick Jagger. And everyone else human beings have been and can be.

When considering Lee, other American tales are remembered: Scott and Zelda, Marilyn, the Kennedys, James Dean: dreamers, and purveyors, of the dream, who, like Icarus, found themselves a bit too close to the sun.

Jesus, Alexander the Great, Joan of Arc, and, yes, Bruce Lee died young enough to believe that there was something about themselves that they *had* to develop, and about the world that *had* to be changed. As we mature, some of us come to another understanding. We hope to recognize things as they are, and to accept them.

Yet, as a species, we ache for saviors. And this is understandable: it's a damned hard world. There's so much each of us wishes we could be liberated from, every single moment of our lives: mortality, morbidity, pain, unrequited dreams. Among the most common saviors our species has developed: work, athletics, family, lovers, social clubs, institutions, philosophies, science, political leaders, storytelling, religions, idols, art, ourselves.

Should human beings survive for a couple hundred more years, I believe that our fame-driven century will have spawned several arrogant American gods: Muhammad Ali, Elvis Presley, and Bruce Lee.

Once *the* spokesperson for self-actualization, Ali has lived plenty (and been beaten up enough) to recognize the myopia of that youthful, basically American religion. Ali's own weighty yet gentle myth has become this: No one, not even The Greatest of All Times, can defy gravity.

"The man who talks about the Tao does not know the Tao," wrote Chuang Tzu.

"Things people praise me for, I didn't do those myself," I've heard the older Ali say. "We don't choose to draw air into our own lungs. We don't decide where we're born or who we are."

Says Lewis, "When I first met Bruce, he told me, 'Joe, I'm not a master. I'm a student. I'm learning, evolving. I don't call myself a master. I'm a student master.'

"I like that," Lewis says, laughing, "'a student master.' And I'm sorry that Bruce seemed to lose that sense of proportion."

"There was nothing wrong with Bruce that a few years wouldn't have fixed," Stirling Silliphant says. "If he'd lived, I think he would've become a genuinely great man."

Two interesting translations of the Chinese word "Lee": 1—natural justice; 2—organic pattern.

Maybe the most resonant Bruce Lee myth is that he was murdered by his own ambition, by his arrogance in believing that he could create himself, an arrogance that, as he aged, he surely would have largely outgrown (a pretty good argument, perhaps, that our world-society, in its Hollywood influenced "wisdom," could be *youth-anizing* itself).

I use no way as way, have no limitation as limitation.

A more poignant epitaph for our century would be difficult to find.

Thirty-two

THIS ALSO MATTERS: At dusk on a September evening in 1973 I stepped blinking into a nickel-and-dime movie house in a village in the mountains of North Carolina. And in that large, dark, warm room where dreams prowl, there was a shock in seeing him.

For the next ninety-three minutes, everything was as blinding, noisy, and insanely beautiful as digitally enhanced film of a nuclear weapons blast.

At the end of *Enter the Dragon,* when I walked from the Banner Elk "Bijou," everything seemed different—brilliant, interesting, as vivid as a just-sliced orange on a winter windowsill. And it stayed that way.

Sitting here now, all these years later, staring yet again at a couple of autographed photos of Lee, I still see heat and light around him. I feel startled by his presence.

And I recognize his scared-shitless fear. Walking across the room to study his ghost on a video screen, I see him working, *oh so hard* to hide it (both from us and from himself), but it's there.

Bone-freezing fear. The stuff every one of us feels in the pit of his or her belly. It's difficult to overstate what it makes us do.

191

Say no, say yes, get married and divorced, write books, jump around in prize rings (and not). Start wars, heal the sick, become saints, say we believe in cosmic charity. Join the National Rifle Association, vote Republican, become "special prosecutors." Create more efficient ways to pummel one another, hold memorial services, etch our names on tombstones.

Design our gods to look a whole lot like us.

Make movies in which we pretend to be invulnerable. Believe that fame itself—the pure, shining twentieth-century god—will make us immortal.

Almost thirty years after being tugged from his shell, Fetus remains grateful to Bruce Lee. Through Lee and Ali (and in reaction to my own fear), I came to train, not only to become an athlete, but a person. I became open to the possibilities and to the mysteries, to the rhythms of life. Frightening though they are.

People climb mountains not because the mountains are there, but to feel a sense of greater connection. Through Lee, I climbed a few mountains, then knew that I was connected. And I could believe, for a time, that I was less afraid. Today, at forty-seven, I don't feel that our mentors can do much more for us than that.

About the Author

Davis Miller is the author of the nonfiction novel *The Tao of Muhammad Ali* (Three Rivers Press, October 1999). His first published story, "My Dinner with Ali," was judged to be the best essay published in an American newspaper magazine in 1989. A shorter version of "My Dinner with Ali" was a finalist for the 1990 National Magazine Award and in 1999 was judged by David Halberstam to be one of the fifty best pieces of sports writing of the twentieth century. The short version of "My Dinner with Ali" has been anthologized in *The Best American Sports Writing of the Century* (Houghton Mifflin, 1999) and in *The Muhammad Ali Reader* (Ecco Press, 1998). His nonfiction short story "The Zen of Muhammad Ali" was nominated for the 1994 Pulitzer Prize for feature writing. "The Zen of Muhammad Ali" was anthologized in *The Best American Sports Writing, 1994* (Houghton Mifflin, 1994). Miller is at work on several books, including a memoir called *So May It Secretly Begin,* a novel, a collection of short fiction and nonfiction, a novella, and a nonfiction novel about Marvin Gaye. He has two children, Johanna and Isaac, and lives near Winston-Salem, North Carolina, where he was born.